DATE DUE

THE SUPREME COURT AND
SOVEREIGN STATES

LONDON : HUMPHREY MILFORD

Oxford University Press

THE SUPREME COURT AND SOVEREIGN STATES

By CHARLES WARREN

Formerly Assistant Attorney General of the
United States (1914–1918) and author of
"The Supreme Court in United States History"

PRINCETON

PRINCETON UNIVERSITY PRESS

1924

The Princeton University Press, Princeton New Jersey

CONTENTS

THE SUPREME COURT AND
SOVEREIGN STATES

Although educated and brought up a soldier, and probably having been in as many battles as anyone else, certainly in as many as most people could have taken part in, yet there was never a time nor a day when it was not my desire that some just and fair way should be established for settling difficulties, instead of bringing innocent persons into conflict and withdrawing from productive labor able-bodied men, who, in a large majority of cases, have no particular interest in the subject over which they are contending. I look forward to a day when there will be courts established that shall be recognized by all nations, which will take into consideration all differences between nations, and settle, by arbitration or decision of such courts, these questions.

Letter of General Ulysses S. Grant to the Universal Peace Union, December, 1879.

THE CONFEDERATION AND
THE CONSTITUTION

IN the year 1847, a noted New York lawyer, John Van Buren, arguing one of the great cases in our history—involving the power of a State to legislate with reference to immigrants, urged the Court to hasten its decision, as some of the immigrants held in quarantine by New York officials were dying; and said he, with irony, "it would be a consolation to their friends to know that they were *dying constitutionally*."

It is the duty of American citizens, especially of those just going forth into American life, to consider more carefully than in the past, how they are *living, constitutionally*—to understand the principles, to note the manner of operation, and to apply the lessons of our American Constitution. To do this, something more is required than a knowledge of the law and of governmental institutions of the country. The origins of the Constitution, not merely as a political document, but as the work of human beings, must be known.

Long ago, old Thomas Fuller quaintly said, in 1655: "We live in a troublesome age, and he needs to have a soft bed who can sleep nowadays amidst so much loud noise and impetuous rumours. Wherefore it seemeth to me both a safe and cheap receipt to procure quiet and repose to the mind that complains of want of rest to prescribe the reading of History. Great is the pleasure and profit thereof." To understand the Constitution, we must first travel along the road of history—perhaps, not to secure Fuller's "quiet and repose to the mind"—possibly, not for the "pleasure thereof"—but, indubitably, for the "profit thereof." For, said James Howell, one of Fuller's contemporaries, there is in history, "that great treasury of time and promptuary of heroique actions . . . rich and copious matter to raise discourse upon." Not only is the past of use in elucidating the problems of the present, but the value of the past lies also in the future; for "we should measure that which has been done by what it makes us do."

The great function of the Supreme Court of the United States, in adjudicating controversies between sovereign States of the Union, has its roots in history. The growth of this function has helped to form the nation; and, as with the ancient Hebrews, much of our history is to be found in the Book of Judges— "The Lord raised up Judges which delivered them out of the hand of those that despoiled them." The lessons of this function of the Court may be of service beyond the limits of the United States.

For an understanding of this function of the

THE CONSTITUTION

Supreme Court, one must go back to the year 1781, when thirteen, separate, independent, sovereign American States finally adopted a framework of government—the Articles of Confederation—which contained, amongst other provisions, one entirely new expedient of statecraft.[1] It is sometimes forgotten today how independent and sovereign the States actually were and regarded themselves, one hundred and forty-three years ago. A few contemporary instances are enlightening. Thus, Connecticut, in its statute adopting a declaration of rights and privileges in 1776, declared itself a "Republic" which "shall forever be and remain a free, sovereign and independent State"; Massachusetts, in its Constitution of 1780, declared itself "a free, sovereign and independent body politic or state by the name of the Commonwealth of Massachusetts." Samuel Adams used to write of the "Republic of Massachusetts Bay."[2] The booksellers advertised for sale in the newspapers copies of "The Constitutions of the several Independent States of America." General Henry Knox (a most ardent Federalist) in drafting the frame for the Society of the Cincinnati in 1783, spoke of the war as having resulted in the establishment of the Colonies as "Free, Independent and Sovereign States." In the treaty of peace, Great Britain acknowledged the United States, naming each State separately, to be "free, sovereign and independent States." The State

[3]

Courts, and later the early Federal Courts, used similar language. The Pennsylvania Legislature recited, in a statute of December 3, 1782, that "whereas by the separation of the thirteen United States from Great Britain, the Commonwealth of Pennsylvania hath become a sovereign and independent State, and in consequence of such separation, a government established solely on the authority of the people hath been formed."[3]

But these independent and sovereign States, which were unitedly fighting a prolonged war, realized that when the war closed there were serious domestic controversies between themselves, which had been pending or which had arisen during the war, and as to which some method of settlement must be found, if they were to preserve their independence. John Jay wrote to Gerry: "In my opinion, few things demand more immediate care than this subject. At present, a sense of common danger guarantees our union; we have neither the time nor inclination to dispute among ourselves. Peace will give us leisure, and leisure often finds improper occasions for employment."[4]

It was Benjamin Franklin, who made the first suggestion, as early as 1775, that a Congress representing the States should have power of "settling all disputes and differences between colony and colony about limits or any other cause if such should arise"; but it was John Dickinson of Delaware, who, on July 12,

[4]

1776, eight days after the Declaration of Independence, proposed the clause in the Articles of Confederation, which, five years later, was adopted by the States, individually, as a possible means of settling their controversies.[5] These Articles provided that each State should, by its voluntary agreement, relinquish the exercise of certain powers of sovereignty inherent in it as an independent State, namely the powers of engaging in war and of entering into any treaty, confederation or alliance without the consent of Congress, and that for "all disputes and differences" between the States, arising from any cause whatever, the United States in Congress assembled, as "the last resort on appeal," should exercise an authority to constitute a Court "to hear and finally determine the controversy"; that for each case, as it arose, the litigant State should name a certain number of persons, from whom "commissioners or judges" should be drawn by lot; and that if any State should neglect to name them, the Congress might do so in its place; these judges were to have power to proceed to judgment and to pronounce a final decree, even if the defendant State refused to appear before them. Thus, for the first time in history, there came into existence a judicial tribunal with compulsory jurisdiction over sovereign States.[6]

In the six years, however, between 1781 when the Articles of Confederation went into operation, and

1787 when the Constitution was framed, there was little opportunity to see whether such a tribunal could be practically effective, for only one controversy was actually tried and decided by a tribunal of judges. But this was one of the utmost seriousness.

During many years, the State of Connecticut had laid claim to large parts of Pennsylvania, comprising what are now Luzerne, Lackawanna, Wyoming and four other counties in Northeastern Pennsylvania—more than 5,000,000 acres, where now are located great anthracite coal mines and iron and oil lands, and in which lie the cities of Scranton, Wilkes-Barre, and Franklin.[7] Before the Revolution, settlers under grants from Connecticut had taken possession of these lands and there had been armed conflict with Pennsylvania citizens. So alarmed had Congress been that, in 1776, it formally urged that hostilities cease and that Connecticut desist from introducing more settlers. Finally, within eight months after the Articles of Confederation were ratified, Pennsylvania had sought to lay her case before the new tribunal provided for by those Articles; a Court was duly appointed by Congress, and on November 12, 1782, the Court convened in the city of Trenton, to pass upon the respective claims of two sovereign States.[8] One month later, the Court pronounced "their sentence or judgment" in favor of Pennsylvania. (See Appendix A.)

"The international significance of this strange and

novel experience of a State appearing against a State in a Court of justice was not lost upon the public men of the day."[9] Robert R. Livingston, then Secretary of Foreign Affairs of the Confederation, writing to Lafayette, said: "It is a singular event. There are few instances of independent States submitting their cause to a Court of justice. The day will come, when all disputes in the great republic of Europe will be tried in the same way, and America be quoted to exemplify the wisdom of the measure." The Pennsylvania State Council published a resolution saying that the decision "promised the happiest consequences to the Confederacy, as an example was thereby set of two contending sovereignties adjusting their differences in a Court of justice, instead of involving themselves and perhaps their confederates in war and bloodshed." And a Philadelphia newspaper made the following interesting comment, which has hitherto been unnoted by historians:

This celebrated case, whose decision has been had under the ninth resolution of the Articles of Confederation presents to the world a new and extraordinary spectacle. Two powerful and popular States, sovereign and independent (except as members of the federal union) contending for a tract of country equal in extent to many, and superior to some, European kingdoms. Instead of recurring to arms, the *ultima ratio* of kings and States, they submit to

[7]

the arbitration of judges mutually chosen from in-different States. The merits of their pretensions are examined by the rules of reason, and judgment framed upon the testimony of records and public documents, illustrated and enforced by the arguments of learned and ingenious men, and in the space of forty days a decree given ascertaining the right of these important claims. The expense has not exceeded what has been often incurred in disputes of private property even in this country. Nothing is wanting to complete the honour and happiness of the United States on this event but a cheerful, ready acqui-escence in this definite judgment; and it is not doubted but the usual wisdom and prudence of the State of Connecticut will be manifested on this occasion.

The judgment, though pronounced as unanimous, appears in fact to have been arrived at by a three to two vote of the Judges; nevertheless, the leading Con-necticut newspaper said that though "Connecticut has suffered a very great injury in her charter rights by the decision of the high Court at Trenton . . . the decree is final and Connecticut must acquiesce, unless it can be proved that there was some mis-conduct in the proceedings."

The foregoing illustrates how simply the States and the people of the day accepted the idea that sov-ereign States might and should appear before a Court, even before a Court having compulsory jurisdiction.

[8]

THE CONSTITUTION

It is sometimes said that the experience of the American States with judicial settlement of differences has no bearing on conditions in the modern world, since those States were so similar in character, whereas the nations of the world differ so largely in racial characteristics and economic interests. But we of today tend to lose sight of the fact that while, in the lapse of over a century, the interests of the States have become more or less uniform, and the racial and other differences between their inhabitants have largely disappeared, this happy condition did not prevail in 1787. Then, the differences between the States—economic, social, religious, commercial— were in some instances as great as the differences between many of the nations of Europe today; and out of these differences arose materially hostile and discriminating State legislation. Washington, writing to Lafayette, in 1788, said that it appeared to him, "little short of a miracle that the delegates from so many different States (which States you know are also different from each other in their manners, circumstances and prejudices) should unite in forming a system of National Government." Pierce Butler of South Carolina said, in the Federal Convention, that he considered the interests of the Southern States and of the Eastern States "to be as different as the interests of Russia and Turkey." George Mason, in the Virginia Convention of 1788, spoke of this

[9]

country as "containing inhabitants so very different in manners, habits, and customs."[10]

There were even differences in language between the States. Pennsylvania was practically one-third German. There was a large German population in the lower Counties of South Carolina and in Western Maryland and Northern Virginia; and it may be noted that so greatly was the German language prevalent in this country that, as late as 1794, a motion was made in Congress that the laws of the United States be printed in the German language, in such proportion as the Secretary of State might "think proper and necessary to accommodate the German citizens of the United States"; and a Committee of the House actually reported in favor of this proposal.[11] New York had a large Dutch population, which in some localities were strongly opposed to the English. The Scotch-Irish, who were in many places highly antagonistic to population of English descent, formed nearly one-half of the white population in South Carolina and nearly one-third in Pennsylvania, Delaware, Georgia and North Carolina; so that as late as 1821, General Archibald McNiel said that he was the first man elected to Congress from his District in the interior of North Carolina, who had not been able to canvass in Gaelic. So much for differences in language.[12]

It is sometimes said also that the States in the

1780's were not sovereign in the same manner that nations are. As shown above, they at least considered themselves so sovereign. One further instance is of interest. One of the attributes of a sovereign State is the right to preserve its neutrality in case of dispute between other States. In 1784, New York and Vermont (which was not then a State of the Union) were on the point of war with each other.[12] And a striking example of how sovereign the other States deemed themselves is shown by a hitherto forgotten proclamation then issued by John Hancock, as Governor of Massachusetts, as follows:

Whereas an unhappy dispute has subsisted between some of the citizens of the State of New York and the people inhabiting the territory called the New Hampshire Circuits or State of Vermont, and it being probable from the present disposition of the parties that the same controversy may be recommenced, to the great distress and calamity of all concerned therein, and there being great reason to fear that some citizens of the Commonwealth who live on the borders of the said State of Vermont may, by uncautiously intermeddling with the contention, involve themselves and families in that distress which is at all times the consequence of civil dissentions, unless care is taken to prevent it.

I have, therefore, at the request of the General Court, thought fit to issue this Proclamation, commanding and enjoining it upon all the citizens of this Commonwealth that in all and every controversy now existing or that may hereafter exist between the citizens of New York and the people inhabiting the new State, or between any of them, in whatever form or manner the same may exist, they, the citizens of this Commonwealth, conduct themselves according to the strictest rules of neutrality, and that they give no aid or assistance to either party, but that those who live on the borders of the said State and within this Commonwealth sell to each party indifferently such things as they have to sell without giving preference to either; that they send no provisions, arms, or ammunition or other necessities to a fortress or garrison besieged by either party. And all the citizens and inhabitants of this commonwealth are absolutely and most solemnly forbidden to take arms in support of or engaging in the service or contributing to the conquest, success, or defence of either of the said parties, as they will answer it at their peril.

This proclamation, not only in matter but even in phraseology, is substantially similar, so far as it goes, to the neutrality proclamations issued by the United States as a sovereign nation, towards the belligerent sovereign nations, in 1914.

But while these sovereign States had assented to the scheme of a judicial tribunal under the Confederation, the views expressed by the newspapers and by the letters of the day as to its successful operation were too optimistic. There were serious defects in the scheme. It will be seen that, in some ways, the tribunal itself resembled more an arbitration commis-

THE CONSTITUTION

sion than a Court; for it was not a permanent body, being specially chosen for each case after the controversy had reached the boiling point, and the judges were named by each party; furthermore, while it rendered a decree and filed it with Congress, there was no body which had authority to execute or enforce the decree, either on the States or on individuals.

It happened, therefore, first: that a State having a dispute lacked confidence in the impartiality of judges, chosen for temporary purposes from lists submitted by the State's opponents. Thus, a New York newspaper intimated that the decision in the Pennsylvania case was influenced by the fact that while that State had paid her quota of the impositions levied by Congress to pay the Continental debt and expenses, Connecticut had neglected to do so.[13] Secondly, the lack of any obligation on the part of a State to comply with the Court's judgment, and the lack of any power in Congress to enforce such judgment, discouraged resort to the court.[14]

Accordingly, while the mere fact of the existence of the Court induced a few States to settle their disputes by compact, and without litigation, most of the boundary conflicts remained unsettled.[15] And it was realized that some stronger means must be found of dealing with such State controversies.

There were also many controversies arising out of other subject matters, which, in their bitterness, were increasingly endangering the peace and welfare of the Confederacy. New York and Virginia were imposing embargoes and import and export duties on products of their sister States. Connecticut was closing her Courts to citizens of Massachusetts, because her own citizens were by the operation of the latter's Tender Law deprived of debts due from Massachusetts debtors. Rhode Island and Connecticut were passing retaliatory legislation excluding citizens of each other from the Courts, because of the former's paper money laws. Pennsylvania Courts were making reprisals on citizens of Virginia.[16]

Everywhere were jealousy, distrust, and commercial warfare. Congress had no power to maintain a national government, by enforcing either its own statutes or the decrees of its Courts. As Edmund Randolph succinctly stated: "Government by supplication cried aloud for reform." Governmental atrophy seemed almost complete.[17]

A remedy must be found, and Burke's words as to the British Revolution of 1688 were applicable to the situation in America one hundred years later.[18]

Ill would our ancestors . . . have deserved their fame for wisdom if they had found no security for their freedom, but in rendering their government feeble in its operations, and precarious in its tenure; if they had been able to contrive no better remedy against arbitrary power than civil confusion.

THE CONSTITUTION

For four months through the hot summer of 1787, fifty-five men sat in Convention in Philadelphia, seeking the remedy.[19] Fortunately, they did not meet in the mood of those of whom Dryden wrote that:

> All in vain our reasoning prophets preach,
> To those whom sad experience ne'er could teach,
> Who can commence new broils in bleeding scars,
> And fresh remembrance of intestine wars.

They thoroughly realized, from their experience, that they must find and establish a firm and united government, with adequate power of self-support, and especially that they must devise some method of settling disputes between the States, if there was to be peace on the American continent. The "spectre of turmoil" was before them in all their debates on the Constitution. It is because they found the remedy in a new form of government, having real legislative and executive power, and having also a permanent judicial tribunal with compulsory jurisdiction over sovereign States, that their action can never be too often impressed upon men of today.

The Federal Convention should be of particular interest to progressive Americans; for it was a Convention of comparatively young men; six of the fifty-five were under thirty-one years of age (the baby of the Convention being Nicholas Gilman of New Hampshire, aged twenty-five); forty-one men

[15]

were under fifty years of age; only three men were over sixty (Dr. Franklin being the oldest with his eighty-one years of honorable and valuable service to his country and to mankind).

To college graduates, and especially to those of Princeton, it should be of particular interest; for nine of these fifty-five men (or one sixth of the whole Convention), including such noted men as Madison, Ellsworth, Paterson and Luther Martin, were graduates of Princeton.[20]

It has been the habit of most historians to glorify these framers of the Constitution so that they have taken the aspect of demigods, or at the least of mere characters of history. Many of the contemporary newspapers yielded to exaggeration in describing them. Thus, said one, "such a body of enlightened and honest men never before met for political purposes in any country upon the face of the earth"; and other papers said that "no age or country ever saw more wisdom, patriotism, and probity united in a single assembly"; and another said, "the wisdom of the continent is now concentered, as it was, in the present convention."[21]

But while its ranks included many men of the highest order of statesmanship, the Convention was like other human institutions, and contained also men of less ability and disinterestedness. And it makes the Convention of greater human interest for us, if we realize that its members received their full share of criticism in their own day. Thus, a contemporary Massachusetts writer, antifederalist in politics, charged the Convention with being composed of "advocates of the British system," and that "the political maneuvres of some of them have always sunk in the vortex of private interest; and that the immense wealth of others has set them above all principle"; and a historian of that day, also an antifederalist, wrote: "This Convention was composed of some gentlemen of the first character and abilities; of some men of shining talents and doubtful character; some of them were uniform republicans; other decided monarchists, with a few neutrals ready to join the strongest party."[22] And a writer in a New York paper said:

We are frequently informed . . . that the present convention . . . is composed of the wisest and best characters in the United States and that it is next to high treason to lisp a suspicion that such a band of patriots can possibly recommend any system or measure, inconsistent with the liberty, interest and happiness of these whom they represent. I am sensible that there are many such characters in that honorable assembly as those writers have mentioned; but, at the same time, it is well known that there are too many of a very different character—perfect Bashaws (saving a want of power) who would trample on the most sacred rights of the people without the slightest reluctance or remorse—men who are possessed of the highest opinion of their own superlative excellence and importance and who have worked themselves into a belief that Heaven hath formed the bulk of mankind to be mere slaves and vassals to men of their superior genius, birth and fortune.

It adds to our appreciation of the difficulty, as well as of the greatness, of their work, when we realize that those who framed the Constitution were subject to the same interests, the same jealousies, the same insistence on retention of State sovereignties, which may confront representatives of nations who may meet today. Let us, therefore, pay some attention to the human side of the preparation of that great document. One light touch is given to the Convention when we read, in a letter of Benjamin Franklin, that it opened with a dinner given by him to the members, at which a cask of porter just received from London "was broached and its contents met with the most cordial reception and approbation. In short, the company agreed unanimously that it was the best porter they had ever tasted."[23] The most prominent members of the Convention, Madison, Hamilton, Rutledge, Pinckney, Mason, Alexander Martin, Hugh Williamson, William Pierce, and some others all lodged at the Indian Queen Tavern—"a large pile of buildings with many spacious halls and numerous small apartments . . . kept in an elegant

[18]

style," and located only two blocks from the Hall
where the Convention sat. A Club of members frequently met here, and also at the City Tavern, for
dinner with General Washington.

That the members did not lack for diversion during
their four months of arduous and supremely important work, may be seen from contemporary newspapers and from the diary kept by George Washington, from which it appears that dinners, teas, excur-
sions into the country, concerts and theatres were of
frequent occasion. Thus, Washington's entries show
that he dined out (and took tea later) on an average
of five afternoons each week; that he dined at a Club
in the suburbs each Saturday, and made frequent
trips to the countryside; that he attended several
concerts, and two plays, "The Tempest or the In-
chanted Island," and "The Crusade or the Generous
Sultan"; that he reviewed troops; went out to Valley
Forge; inspected a steel works; twice went trout fish-
ing; attended high mass "at the Romish Church";
twice dined with the Society of the Cincinnati; and
once with the City Light Horse, the Agricultural Society, and the Sons of St. Patrick. It may also be noted
that on the day when the great debate over the slave
trade occurred, William Samuel Johnson noted in
his diary that he witnessed what was one of the
earliest trial trips of the first steamboat, then just
invented by John Fitch.

[19]

One event may be especially noted. Shortly after the opening of the Convention, Washington attended a lecture on the "Power of Elocution" by a "lady in reduced circumstances," in the course of which there were read extracts from the poems of the great Oriental scholar and the eminent lawyer, Sir William Jones;[24] and then undoubtedly Washington heard and pondered on those great lines from the *Ode in Imitation of Alcaeus*, so often since quoted, but then just written by Jones:

What constitutes a State?
. . . Men, high-minded men:
. . . Men who their duties know,
But know their rights, and knowing, dare maintain,
. . . .
And sovereign law, that State's collected will,
O'er thrones and globes elate,
Sits empress, crowning good, repressing ill.

How strikingly appropriate these lines, when we recall that it was this very "sovereign law, the State's collected will," which those assembled in Philadelphia were seeking to establish!

That the members themselves thoroughly appreciated the momentous character of the work before them is clearly shown in contemporary documents.[25] Thus the delegates from North Carolina wrote home at an early date:

THE CONSTITUTION

A very large field presents to our view, without a single straight or eligible road that has been trodden by the feet of nations. An union of sovereign States, preserving their civil liberties and connected together by such tyes as to preserve permanent and effective governments, is a system not described; it is a circumstance that has not occurred in the history of men; if we shall be so fortunate as to find this description, our time will have been well spent. Several gentlemen of the Convention have their wives here, and other gentlemen have sent for them. This seems to promise a summer's campaign.

George Mason of Virginia wrote to his son:

America has certainly upon this occasion drawn forth her first characters; there are upon this Convention many gentlemen of the most respectable abilities; and, so far as I can discover, of the purest intentions; the eyes of the United States are turned upon this assembly, and their expectations raised to a very anxious degree. May God grant we may be able to gratify them by establishing a wise and just government. For my own part, I never before felt myself in such a situation, and declare I would not, upon pecuniary motives, serve in this Convention for a thousand pounds per day. The revolt from Great Britain and the formation of our new government at that time were nothing, compared with the great business before us. There was then a certain degree of enthusiasm which inspired and supported the mind; but, to view through the calm, sedate medium of reason, the influence which the establishments now proposed may have upon the happiness or misery of millions yet unborn, is an object of such magnitude as absorbs, and in a manner suspends, the operation of the human understanding.

"They have a great work and many difficulties, before them. To form a generous plan of power for thirteen State sovereignties requires the most consummate wisdom," said a contemporary newspaper.

The Convention sat in the State House (Independence Hall), upstairs over the room to the east of the central hallway. It sat every week day, from May 25, to September 17, with but two recesses (one of three days and one of ten); and its sessions lasted from four to seven hours each day.[26]

Of the first meeting of the Convention, a Philadelphia correspondent wrote: "Perhaps this city affords the most striking picture that has been exhibited for ages. Here at the same moment, the collective wisdom of the continent deliberates upon the extensive politics of the confederated empire; two religious conventions clear and distribute the streams of religion throughout the American world; and those veterans whose valour accomplished a mighty revolution are once more assembled to recognize their fellowship in arms and to communicate to their distressed brethren the blessings of peace."[27] (The last reference is to the fact that, five days after the Convention met, the meeting of the General Society of the

[22]

Cincinnati (at which Washington had been re-elected President-General) adjourned, on May 19.)

The proceedings, by vote of the Convention, were secret; and so cautious were the members that visitors to the Hall reported that "sentries are planted without and within to prevent any person from approaching near, who appear to be very alert in their duty," and that "all debate is suspended on the entrance of their own inferior officers."[28] To prevent any disturbance of the debate, by rattling of wheels, the city authorities had caused the pavement of Chestnut Street to be covered with earth. So well was the secrecy preserved that an examination of contemporary newspapers fails to disclose a single item giving a correct report of any portion of the document agreed upon—although several papers published amusingly false accounts of alleged action.[29]

At first, the members were extremely sanguine as to a prompt success in their work, so that a prominent Philadelphian, Benjamin Rush, wrote to a friend:

Dr. Franklin exhibits daily a spectacle of transcendant benevolence by attending the Convention punctually and even taking part in its business and deliberation. He says "it is the most august and respectable Assembly he ever was in in his life," and adds, that he thinks "they will soon finish their business, as there are no prejudices to oppose, nor errors to refute, in any of the body." Mr. Dickinson (who is one of them) informs me that they are all *united* in their objects, and he expects they will be equally united in the means of attaining them.

And a newspaper correspondent wrote with equal confidence:

The present Convention is happily composed of men who are qualified from education, experience and profession for the great business assigned to them. These gentlemen are assembled at a most fortunate period . . . with a variety of experiments before them of the feebleness, tyranny and licentiousness of our American forms of government. Under such circumstances it will not be difficult for them to frame a Federal Constitution that will suit our country.

This initial optimism gave rise to early reports in the papers as to the harmony of the Convention: "Great is the unanimity we hear that prevails in the Convention upon all great federal subjects that it has been proposed to call the room in which they assemble, Unanimity Hall," said the Pennsylvania papers at the end of June.[30] The secrecy of the debates fostered this mistaken report.[31] Yet at the very time of these publications, the Convention had become the scene of determined dissension; and it seemed impossible that the divergent views of the large and the small States, or of New England, the Middle States and the South, or of the commercial and agricultural classes could ever be reconciled or compromised.[32] So that Washington wrote to Alexander Hamilton:

When I refer you to the state of the counsel which prevailed at the period you left the city (some ten days before) and add that they are now, if possible, in a worse train than ever, you will find but little ground on which the hope of a good establishment can be formed. In a word, I almost despair of seeing a favorable issue to the proceedings of our Convention, and do therefore repent having had any agency in the business. . . . I am sorry you went away. I wish you were back. The crisis is equally important and alarming.

And a month later (August 15), Oliver Ellsworth said in the Convention: "We grow more and more sceptical as we proceed. If we do not decide soon, we shall be unable to come to any decision." "Believe me, Sir," wrote Alexander S. Martin to Governor Caswell of North Carolina, "it is no small task to bring to a conclusion the great objects of a United Government, viewed in different points by thirteen independent sovereignties."[33] Nevertheless, in spite of their serious differences, members were quoted as saying "scarcely a personality or offensive expression escaped during the whole session."[34]

That the country was anxiously anticipating the outcome of the Convention is remarkably shown in numerous letters and articles in the papers of the day. "The eyes of the whole continent are now cast on that respectable body, the Convention. The heart of every American, good or bad, must be interested in the result of their deliberation," wrote a correspondent from the South. "The present time is a very important one. The eyes of friends and enemies, of all Europe, nay of the whole world, are upon the United States," wrote one from New York. And another wrote: "The grand convention will certainly be of the highest importance to the political existence and welfare of the United States." "On their detemination alone, and our acquiescence, depends our future happiness and prosperity," wrote one from Virginia. "Our future political safety and happiness depends on the results of their present deliberations," wrote a Pennsylvanian. A Connecticut correspondent wrote that "our impatience to know what the Grand Convention are about . . . has made us snappish." Another wrote in a Philadelphia paper: "It is hoped, from the universal confidence reposed in this delegation, that the minds of the people throughout the United States are prepared to receive with respect, and to try with a fortitude and perseverance, the plan which will be offered to them by men distinguished for their wisdom and patriotism." "Private letters from Europe mention that the oppressed and persecuted in every country look with great eagerness to the United States in the present awful crisis of their affairs," many papers reported.[35]

Many times during its four months session, it seemed inevitable that the Convention would break up, without achieving its purpose; but, each time, a brave spirit of compromise tided over the crisis. Meanwhile, thirteen of the fifty-five members left Philadelphia, owing to illness, discouragement, or pressure of business, professional, or other political duties.[36]

Finally, however, on Saturday, September 15, 1787, delegates representing all the States, save Rhode Island, voted to adopt the final draft of the Constitution. A Philadelphia newspaper correspondent added a vivid touch, by writing: "Having stepped into a beer-house on Saturday evening last, I perceived the room filled with a number of decent tradesmen, who were conversing very freely about the members of the Federal Convention—who, it was said, like good workmen, had finished their work on a Saturday night."[37]

On Monday, September 17, thirty-eight men affixed their signatures to the immortal document; one, duly authorized, signed the name of an absent member. George Washington's signature was accompanied with a remark, reported by the newspapers (but not by Madison in his *Notes*) as follows: "The illustrious Washington was called on by the Convention

[27]

to ratify the Constitution as its President—holding the pen, after a short pause, he pronounced these words too remarkable to be forgotten or unknown: 'Should the States reject this excellent Constitution, the probability is an opportunity will never offer to cancel another—the next will be drawn in blood.' "
Although Dr. Franklin had urged that if there was any member who shared with him some objection to the draft, such member should "doubt a little of his own infallibility" and should yield his signature, in the common interest, there were, nevertheless, three delegates who refused to sign. As those forty-one men came down the steps of Independence Hall, and prepared to return to their homes, it would be interesting to know how accurately they estimated the potency of their four months' work. One man, we know, went back to his lodgings and entered in his diary his view of the event. This is what George Washington wrote, that evening:

Sept. 17, 1787. Met in Convention, when the Constitution received the unanimous consent of eleven States and of Colonel Hamilton from New York, the only delegate from thence in Convention, and was subscribed to by every member present, except Governor Randolph and Colonel Mason from Virginia, and Mr. Gerry from Massachusetts. The business being thus closed, the members adjourned to the City Tavern, dined together, and took a cordial leave of each other. After which, I returned to my lodgings, did some business with, and received the papers from the Secretary of the Convention, and retired to meditate on the momentous work which had been executed.

It was indeed a "momentous work which had been executed"; and it was so recognized by the public of the day—both by its advocates and opponents. Of the manner of its reception a Philadelphia correspondent wrote: "I was walking the other day in Second Street and observed a child of five or six years old, with a paper in his hand, and lisping with a smile, 'Here's what the Convention have done.' Last evening, I was walking down Arch Street and was struck with the appearance of an old man whose head was covered with hoary locks and whose knees bent beneath the weight of it, stepping to his seat by the door, with a crutch in one hand, and his spectacles and the Federal Constitution in the other. These incidents renewed in my mind, the importance of the present era to one half the world! I was pleased to see all ages anxious to know the result of the deliberation of that illustrious Council whose constituents are designed to govern a World of Freemen. The unthinking youth who cannot realize the importance of government seems to be impressed with a sense of our want of system and union; and the venerable sire who is tottering to the grave feels new life at the prospect of having everything valuable secured to posterity."[38] Well was the instrument termed by another newspaper a "revolution in government, accompanied by reasoning and deliberation—an event that has never occurred since the formation of society." And well did still another say that the Convention had laid "America under such obligations to them, for their long, painful and disinterested labour to establish her liberty upon a permanent basis, as no time will ever cancel."

It is that portion of the work of the framers of the Constitution which dealt with one of the great functions of the Supreme Court, with which this present book is concerned.

II

THE SUPREME COURT AND
INTER-STATE SUITS

THE Virginia delegation to the Federal Convention had traits of the diplomats of Great Britain; they arrived on the field first, and they brought with them a fully developed plan for a Constitution.[39] Hence, naturally, it was their plan (probably drafted by James Madison and presented by Governor Edmund Randolph) which became the basis of the final draft of the Constitution.[40] From the clause, which it contained, providing for a Supreme Court with jurisdiction to determine questions "which may involve the national peace and harmony," there was developed Article III of the Constitution as finally adopted, setting forth more specifically the various controversies over which the Court should have jurisdiction—and thus there appeared, for the first time in history, the provision for a permanent Supreme Court with compulsory jurisdiction over "controversies between two or more States."

"And now is accomplished," said James Wilson in the Pennsylvania Convention, "what the great mind of Henry IV had in contemplation—a system of government for large and respectable dominions,

united and bound together in peace, under a superintending head by which all their differences may be
accommodated without the destruction of the human
race."[41]

We Americans are now so accustomed to the Supreme Court and its peculiar place in our government, that we fail to realize what an absolute novelty
the Federal Convention in 1787 was proposing for
adoption by the people of the States. Never before in
history had there existed a Court with the powers
which this new tribunal was to exercise. For the first
time, there now came into existence a permanent
Court, which should have the power to summon before it sovereign States in dispute and to determine
their respective rights by a judgment which should
be enforceable against them.

Such a Court, with such functions, is the most original, the most distinctively American contribution to
political science to be found in the Constitution. It is
even more. It is the cement which has fixed firm the
whole Federal structure. Or, to change the metaphor
and to use Jefferson's quaint words: "They are setting up a kite to keep the henyard in order."[42]

Undoubtedly, the idea of such a Court is traceable
somewhat to the familiarity of the Colonists with
the various political and judicial committees of the
British Privy Council, which had in the past given
advisory opinions to the King in settlement of

boundary and territorial disputes between the Colonies. Yet the uniqueness of such a Court may be realized, when it is recalled that Hamilton and Madison, with all their broad knowledge of past governmental institutions, were not able, in writing *The Federalist*, to cite anything more similar as a precedent than an old tribunal which existed in the Holy Roman Empire, in 1495, and which was a far cry from the United States Supreme Court.[43]

Though the homely prophesy made by Francis Hopkinson that, "no sooner will the chicken be hatched but everyone will be for plucking a feather," was fulfilled by the immediate and widespread assault which was made upon every other part of the Constitution, it is to be especially noted that the clause which gave jurisdiction to the Supreme Court over controversies between the States of the new Union received not a breath of opposition. The reason for this was the realization by the States of the danger that lay in any less vigorous expedient. As to this part of the Constitution certainly, the words of John Quincy Adams may be truly applied, that it was "wrung from a reluctant people by grinding necessity."[44]

For a real understanding of the meaning of this extraordinary grant of jurisdiction to the Supreme Court, it is necessary to bear in mind that the Constitution was ratified, *not* by the people of America in their collective capacity—*not* by a nation composed of people in a mass, physically residing within the boundaries of States, but by the people of each State as a separate sovereignty. As James Madison said: "Who are the parties to it? The people. Not the people as composing one great body, but the people as composing thirteen sovereignties." (See Appendix B.)

By such ratification, the sovereign power of each State, i.e., the people of the State, placed a voluntary restriction upon its rights of sovereignty, by granting to the Federal Government the right or power to act on particular matters or by agreeing not to act themselves.[45] So far as it did not relinquish such rights or powers, each State remained then and still remains entirely sovereign.

One of the essential rights of sovereignty, the maintenance of which was surrendered by each State, was that of immunity from suit; when there was granted to the Supreme Court of the United States, the power to summon a State to the bar at the instance of another State, and the power to enter and to enforce its judgments, such a grant constituted a tremendous limitation placed by the State upon its own sovereign freedom.[46] When disputes arise, however, between sovereign States, there are only three known methods by which they can be settled—by war, by agreement (including agreement to arbitrate) or by judicial action. The framers of the Constitution having expressly provided that the individual States should relinquish the exercise of two powers of sovereignty, namely that of making war and that of making compacts (without assent of Congress), there was but one effectual method of settlement of controversies left, namely, the establishment of a Court to judge between the States. The acceptance of such a Court and the surrender of their sovereign right of immunity from compulsory suit constituted the sacrifice which the people of each State were willing to make for the sake of peace and the common welfare.[47]

The significant thing to be noted, however, is that there was nothing harmful, nothing derogatory to a State in such relinquishment of right. Theoretically, a sovereign State is omnipotent, subject to no law of responsibility. Yet such a State has no geographical or historical existence; it is mythical—a state of mind. No State exists in the world which has not relinquished or restricted, by voluntary action, the exercise of some rights, powers or attributes inherent in its absolute sovereignty; for States in a world community cannot afford to insist on absolute rights.

In fact, the degree to which States relax such insistence connotes the progress of civilization and justice. International treaties consist of agreements by which two nations waive such insistence, in behalf of peace and mutual welfare. For instance, no sovereign right of a country can be more absolute than that of maintaining fortifications in its own territories. Yet the United States has relinquished the exercise of such right, by agreements with Great Britain not to fortify its Canadian boundaries, and with Japan, England and France (in the famous Four Power Treaty) not to fortify its islands in the Pacific. No sovereign right is more perfect than the freedom from any obligation to maintain the rights or boundaries of another nation, or than freedom from obligation to defend any other Nation. Yet the United States, by treaty with New Granada (now Columbia) in 1846, solemnly imposed upon itself an obligation to guarantee the neutrality of the isthmus of Panama and the rights of sovereignty and property which New Granada possessed over it; and in 1904, by a similar treaty the United States guaranteed the independence of Panama. No sovereign right is greater than the exclusive power of a country's courts over persons within the country. Yet, by numerous treaties, the United States has granted to foreign consuls the power to decide judicially on the rights and liabilities of foreigners on ships in our ports, and, in one treaty with France, the United States even granted the power so to decide in *all* suits between Frenchmen in this country.[48]

Much nonsense was talked in 1787 about impairment of sovereignty and State independence; and much similar nonsense is repeated at the present time.[49] The fact is, however, that no action voluntarily entered into by a State can impair its sovereignty. A State may, it is true, relinquish or restrict the exercise of certain rights or powers or prerogatives which it would otherwise have. A free, voluntary act of surrender or restriction cannot, however, be deemed *per se* derogatory to any State; and whether or not it is a wise or desirable action by a State, either through an international treaty or by a compact or otherwise, depends entirely upon the value of the end to be achieved.

It was because the people of the thirteen, independent, sovereign States in America believed that the end to be accomplished—namely, peace and mutual welfare—justified a restriction on the exercise of their sovereignty, justified a surrender of their sovereign right to be immune from suit, that they were willing voluntarily to ratify a Constitution which placed such a restriction and embodied such a surrender.

Such being the causes and conditions which induced the submission by the American States to the compulsory jurisdiction of a Court, let us now consider the extent to which that jurisdiction has been exercised.

It will probably surprise most American citizens

to learn that between 1789 and 1923 in such interstate suits, twenty-seven States of the Union have
appeared as plaintiffs and twenty-three as defend-
ants; and that thirty-seven States have been on one
side or the other of such a suit. There have been
thirty-nine controversies involving eighty-one reported decisions of the Supreme Court. Twenty-six
of these controversies involved disputes as to boundaries or territory; two involved recovery of money due
from a State on its bonds or contracts and eleven
were controversies involving direct injuries alleged
to have been committed by one State to another. (See
Appendix C.)

Evidencing the seriousness of some of these disputes is the fact that in at least four instances—*New
Jersey* v. *New York* in the 1820's; *Missouri* v. *Iowa*
in the 1840's; *Louisiana* v. *Mississippi* in the 1900's;
and *Oklahoma* v. *Texas* in very recent years, armed
conflicts between the militia or citizens of the contending States had been a prelude to the institution of the
suits in the Court. And in several of the other suits,
a state of facts was presented which, if arising between independent nations, might well have been a
cause for war.

The first suit between States did not arise until ten
years after the new government was instituted—
New York and Connecticut being the parties, and the

suit being dismissed for lack of legal interest in New York.[50]

A period of thirty years elapsed before another suit appeared; but in 1829, New Jersey presented to the Court her long standing controversy with New York over her title to and sovereignty over the waters of New York Harbor and Hudson River. This dispute had given rise to much bitterness of feeling and retaliatory legislation between the States; and there had been forcible seizures and practically armed conflict over the rights of various steamboat owners to run their boats upon these waters—so that William Wirt, in arguing the great Steamboat Monopoly Case in 1824, said: "Here are three States almost on the eve of war," and that if the Court did not interpose its friendly hand, "there would be civil war."[51] New York now being sued in the Court, refused to acknowledge the Court's jurisdiction, claiming that until Congress made provision for the method of bringing a defendant State into Court, suit would not lie. This claim Chief Justice Marshall vigorously denied; and acting upon the rule which the Court had laid down in several cases of suits by individuals against a State, he held that the Court had power to proceed *ex parte*, if a refractory State refused to appear when duly summoned. (See Appendix D.) It is interesting to note that this extreme assertion of

State-Rights by New York, occurred just at the time when Calhoun and South Carolina were maintaining their Nullification doctrines, and Georgia was refusing to obey the mandate of the Court in the Cherokee Indian Cases. The boldness of Marshall in maintaining that the Court had the extraordinary power to proceed to adjudge the rights of a sovereign State, even if the latter refused to appear, is an illustration of the potent influence which the Court exerted in establishing the Constitution on a firm basis. The result of this courageous attitude was that New York and New Jersey settled their dispute by a compact assented to by Congress.[52]

Six years later, in 1838, the power of the Court to settle boundary disputes at all was called in question in a suit by Rhode Island against Massachusetts—involving a strip of land on the latter's northern boundary of about 150 square miles, inhabited by 5000 people whose political status as citizens of the one or the other State would be affected by the decision of the case. In an opinion rendered by Judge Henry Baldwin of Pennsylvania, an opinion which is one of the landmarks of American constitutional law, the power of the Court to settle all boundary and territorial disputes between States was definitely affirmed—and this too, even in cases which would be considered as presenting purely political questions, if arising between the nations of Europe or elsewhere.

Though the Court's power was thus decided, Rhode Island finally lost the case on its merits in 1846.[53]

Four years later, a serious boundary conflict between Missouri and Iowa was decided, which involved sovereignty over a valuable strip of territory of about 2000 square miles—a tract about the size of East and West Flanders and about two-thirds the size of Alsace. This controversy had been pending for twelve years; Missouri at one time had called out 1500 troops and Iowa 1100, to defend their respective alleged rights. The conflict of claims was the more serious, by reason of the fact that if Missouri prevailed, these 2000 square miles would become additional slave territory; if Iowa won, they would be free. The Court finally decided in favor of Iowa. Thus, just at a time when the dire question of slavery was threatening the stability of the Union in every political direction, a decision of the Court settled its fate for 2000 square miles of American territory. No wonder that Lewis Cass, Senator from Michigan rose in the Senate, in 1855, and said: "It is a great moral spectacle to see the decree of the Judges of our Supreme Court on the most vital questions obeyed in such a country as this. They determine questions of boundaries between independent States, proud of their character and position, and tenacious of their rights, but who yet submit. They have stopped armed men in our country. Iowa and Mis-

[41]

souri had almost got to arms about their boundary line, but they were stopped by the intervention of the Court. In Europe, armies run lines and they run them with bayonets and cannon. They are marked with ruin and devastation. In our country, they are run by an order of the Court. They are run by an unarmed surveyor with his chain and his compass, and the monuments which he puts down are not monuments of devastation but peaceable ones."

A boundary dispute between Ohio and the Territory of Michigan in 1835 had occasioned actual forcible conflict, known as the Toledo War. Luckily, as one of the parties was a Territory, Congress had power to settle the question and did so by its Act admitting Michigan as a State. Had Michigan been a State, Congress would had no authority in the matter, and without a Supreme Court empowered to intervene, force would have been the only resource for the complaining States.[54]

One other boundary dispute before the Civil War may be mentioned, not because of its importance (as it involved merely the question where the line ran in the Chattahoochee River), but because it shows that the Southern States, though having little confidence at that time in the political branches of the Government, were entirely content to leave the decision of some of their sovereign rights as States to the Supreme Judiciary. Hence, we have the remarkable spectacle of two States who, less than one year from the date of the decision, were to secede from the Union, accepting the decision of a Court under a Constitution which they were so soon to repudiate.

After the close of the Civil War, there came a steady increase in the number of boundary controversies submitted for decision by the Court. Most of these involved changes in the course of rivers or locations of channels or jurisdiction to highwater mark; but important questions as to respective rights of States to tax and to serve process of law depended on their solution. Virginia and Tennessee, however, disputed the ownership of a tract of land 118 miles long and two to eight miles in width on the former's southern boundary. Maryland and West Virginia disputed the sovereignty over about forty miles in Garrett County in Maryland. Virginia and West Virginia disputed the sovereignty of two whole counties—the jag in the northeast corner of the latter State, where Harper's Ferry and Martinsburg are located.

By far the most important boundary case was decided in 1906, brought by Louisiana against Mississippi. This case involved great financial interests—the oyster fisheries in the waters between the two States. The controversy had been pending for ten years; each State had appointed armed patrols, and by law and force had sought to exclude fishermen of the other State. Finally as was stated in the decision, "in view of the danger of an armed conflict," the oyster commissions of the two States adopted a joint resolution establishing a neutral territory, pending a decision of the Supreme Court. The situation was precisely that of an economic conflict in mutually claimed territory, which, if occurring between nations of Europe or elsewhere, would be very probable cause of war. As late as 1909, a suit by the State of Washington against Oregon, involving the channel of the Columbia River presented another inflamed boundary question, the decision of which might leave one or the other State in control of the very valuable salmon fisheries.[55]

From the above summary, it is to be noted that boundary disputes even between the American States do not necessarily involve mere dry questions of title and geographical lines. They may settle serious social and economic relations. It is conceivable that, as between certain of our States, they might, on some occasion, involve even racial questions.

The sources of State controversy, nevertheless, have not been confined to boundaries. More important causes of dispute have existed and are increasingly arising.

As early as 1876, South Carolina sued the State of Georgia on the ground that the latter State was obstructing interstate commerce and diverting waters of the Savannah River from one State into another. The Court held, however, that as Congress had authorized the obstruction, the State had no ground of complaint.

In 1900, a novel and very grave source of dispute was presented in a suit by Louisiana against Texas. The latter State by statute had given to her officials wide powers to enforce very drastic quarantine regulations and to detain vessels, persons and property coming into Texas. In 1899, a health officer of Texas took advantage of a single case of yellow fever in New Orleans to lay an embargo on all commerce between that city and the State of Texas, and this embargo was enforced by armed guards posted at the frontier. Louisiana alleged that the yellow fever case was a mere pretext, that the real motive was to divert commerce from New Orleans to the port of Galveston in Texas, that this was shown by the fact that no embargo was maintained against commerce coming to Galveston from the seriously infected ports of Mexico. Accordingly, Louisiana sought an injunction against Texas and its officials. The Court finally held against Louisiana, but chiefly because (as pointed out in a later case) there was no proof that the action of the particular health officer in question was actually the act of the State. The vital issue had been raised, however, as to the extent to which a sovereign State may manipulate its own domestic laws for the purpose of, or with the necessary result of, inflicting a direct injury on another State. The language of Judge Brown (who dissented) is particularly significant as showing that the source of the dispute, which thus came before the Court for adjudication, was precisely such as, if arising between foreign nations, might occasion a war.

In view of the solicitude which, from time immemorial, States have manifested for the interest of their own citizens; of the fact that wars are frequently waged by States in vindication of individual rights, of which the last war with England, the opium war of 1840 between Great Britain and China, and the war which is now being carried on in South Africa between Great Britain and the Transvaal Republic, are all notable examples . . . it would seem a strange anomaly if a State of this Union, which is prohibited by the Constitution from levying war upon another State, could not invoke the authority of this Court by suit, to raise an embargo which had been established by another State against its citizens and their property.

An embargo, though not an act of war, is frequently resorted to as preliminary to a declaration of war, and may be treated under certain circumstances as a sufficient *casus belli.*

A year later, in 1901, the Court had before it another serious source of State controversy when Mis-

souri filed against Illinois a bill in equity seeking to
enjoin the latter State from diverting the sewage of
Chicago from Lake Michigan into the Illinois River
and eventually so polluting the waters of the Mississippi as to endanger through typhoid germs the
health of the citizens of Missouri. There was thus
presented the grave question of how far one State
could institute a public nuisance, to the detriment of
another. The right of the Court to take jurisdiction
over any such question was vigorously assailed by
Illinois; but the Court sustained its power to act,
and held that if the health and comfort of the inhabitants of a State are so threatened, the State itself
is a proper party to represent them; and, said
Judge Shiras, since diplomatic powers and the right
to make war had been surrendered by Missouri under the Constitution, the duty of providing a remedy
had been performed by giving to the Supreme Court
jurisdiction in such cases. Thus sustaining its power,
the Court, when the case was finally tried on the
evidence, found that Missouri had not proved its
case.

In 1902, a suit by Kansas against Colorado involved a momentous question as to how far a State
by instituting extensive irrigation works within its
boundary could deprive another State of the water
of a non-navigable river flowing from one State
into the other, and could thus reduce much arable

[47]

land in a neighboring State to a desert condition. Kansas sought an injunction, in behalf of its farmers threatened with irreparable loss and injury. The Court held that it had power to settle the dispute, and though it found that Kansas had not proved its case on the facts, it held that the time might come when it would have to intervene to protect the substantial interests of Kansas.

A somewhat similar question was presented in a suit decided in 1922, between Wyoming and Colorado, brought to prevent inordinate diversion and retention in Colorado of the waters of the Laramie River. In this case, the State of Wyoming succeeded in obtaining an injunction.

In 1921, the Court decided a case brought by New York against New Jersey, seeking to enjoin the discharge of the latter's sewage into New York harbor. New York alleged the public nuisance which would result and "the grave injury to the health, to the property and to the commercial welfare of the State and city." That such allegations are sufficient to give to the State a right to sue "is very clear," said the Court, in its decision.[56] As the evidence, however, was not sufficiently clear and convincing, the Court refused the injunctions at that time and suggested that the States try to effect a settlement by agreement.

In 1923, a controversy of extraordinary interest was presented when the States of Pennsylvania and of Ohio, appearing both as owners of property themselves and as representing the rights of their citizens likely to be injured, sought an injunction to restrain West Virginia from enforcing her natural gas law. It appeared that for many years natural gas had been the subject of interstate commerce between these States; and that West Virginia by a recent statute was seeking to give to users of gas within her boundaries a preference or a practical monopoly of all gas developed in West Virginia. Such an interference with interstate commerce, the Court held could not be allowed, and it directed an injunction against the State and its officials; for it said that, if one State had such a power, every State had it, and embargo might be retaliated by embargo, and all commerce might be halted at State lines—the very thing which it was the purpose of the Constitution to prevent.

The latest decision was rendered, in 1923, in a contest between North Dakota and Minnesota. It was claimed that a drainage and ditching system set up by the latter State had flooded the farms of a part of North Dakota, and an injunction and damages of several million dollars were sought. The Court held that the fact alleged presented a clear case of injury by one State to another, which it was within its powers to decide; but here again it found the facts against North Dakota's claim.

There has been one further class of controversy between States which has been held susceptible of decision by the Court, in spite of strenuous contentions against the Court's power to act in such cases.
Could one State sue another to enforce payment of
bonds issued by a State and repudiated by it? In
1904, however, the Court held that the State of
South Dakota, which had become the owner of bonds
of North Carolina, through a gift from the bond-
holders, could sue North Carolina, could recover
the money due, and could foreclose on the security
pledged for payment of the bonds.

Such have been some of the varied questions of
controversy between the States of this Union which
have been actually decided by a Court.

It is to be noted that through all the opinions of
the Court there runs like a golden thread, the con-
sciousness of the Court's great responsibilities and a
realization of the august character of the litigants
before it. No technical rules of practice or of plead-
ing have been permitted (as the Court itself recently
said) to leave "room for the slightest inference that
the more restricted rules applicable to individuals
have been applied to a great public controversy, or
that anything but the largest justice, after the
amplest opportunity to be heard, has in any degree
entered into the case." There must be every opportunity allowed "to guard against the possibility of

[50]

error and thus reach the result most consonant with the honor and dignity of both parties." More than once the Court has proceeded upon the deliberate theory that, as Judge Holmes phrases it, "great States have a temper superior to that of private litigants" and must be dealt with "in the untechnical spirit proper for dealing with a quasi-international controversy."[57]

What living suggestions for the present and for the future, do these somewhat dry historical data as to the Court contain? To answer this question, two facts must be constantly borne in mind. First, that in 1787, thirteen, independent, sovereign States found no difficulty, when the necessities of peace and common welfare impelled, in surrendering the exercise of their sovereign right to be immune from suit and in agreeing to submit all their controversies to a Court of compulsory jurisdiction. Second, that the Supreme Court has never yet been confronted with any class of controversy between States, which it has found itself incapable to decide, as a matter of law and appropriate for judicial determination.

"The bearings of which observation," said the sagacious Jack Bunsby to Captain Cuttle, "the bearings of which observation lays in the application on it."

III

COURTS AND JUSTICIABLE CASES

FROM the foregoing summary of cases it will be noted that the Supreme Court of the United States, when actually faced with a decision in a case between American States, has never yet found any kind of an interstate controversy which it has held itself incapable to decide, although there have been cases in which it held that the facts involved did not permit a judgment in favor of the State bringing the suit.

Several years ago, some misguided jurist thought fit to use the barbarous and tongue-twisting word, "justiciable," to signify the class of cases between States and between nations which were capable of decision by a Court of law; and since then much intellectual effort has been expended by international statesmen, to define what controversies are and what are not "justiciable." The American States, however, have expressly agreed, when they adopted their Constitution, that *all their controversies shall be settled by a Court;* and as Chief Justice Marshall said, long ago, if the States be parties, "it is entirely unimportant what may be the subject of controversy. Be it what it may, these parties have a constitutional right to come into the Courts of the Union."[58]

The Supreme Court has substantially taken the position that, inasmuch as, under the Constitution, the States cannot make war upon each other, they cannot be allowed to do to each other any such act as would be the occasion for war between independent nations. If one State, by its duly authorized agency or official, performs or is about to perform a definite act, to the possible injury of an actual right or interest claimed by another State—that is sufficient to warrant the Court in deciding upon the rights of the two parties.

Hence, even political questions may be involved and may be "justiciable" by the Supreme Court; and it has been well remarked that "not only were question of a political nature not excluded but they were, from the necessities of the case, the very kind of controversies which it must have been primarily the intention of the Constitution to include."[59] It is said, however, that the Supreme Court has held that there is at least one question which it cannot decide and which is a political question, not a judicial one, viz., it cannot decide whether the party sued is or is not a State.[60] But this apparent exception will, on closer examination, prove to be no exception at all. For in a suit by one State against another, there can be no "controversy" involving a decision by the Court as to whether the defendant is or is not a State. The very fact that X State sues Y State, involves the admission by X that Y *is* a State; if Y is not a State,

then all jurisdiction of the suit falls, so far as jurisdiction of the Court depends on the suit being a
"controversy between States." Thus, while this question, which the Court has said is a political one and
therefore incapable of its decision, may easily arise
in a suit between private individuals, it can never
arise in a suit between States; for the mere raising
of the question by a plaintiff State would *ipso facto*
take its case out of Court; and no defendant State
would set up as a defense a denial of its own existence as a State.

The Supreme Court has *power*, therefore, to settle,
as between the States, questions which, between foreign nations, would be known as "non-justiciable."
And for the Supreme Court, a "justiciable question"
means simply a question which the Court decides that
it will settle in any particular case.[61] To quote from
a familiar classic:

"When *I* use a word," Humpty Dumpty said, "it
means just what I choose it to mean, neither more
nor less." "The question is," said Alice, "whether
you *can* make words mean so many different things."
"The question is," said Humpty Dumpty, "which is
to be master—that's all."

But though, at the present time, it is difficult for
one to suggest a real controversy between American
States which the Court would not hold to be "justi-

ciable," it is an important and interesting fact to remember that this breadth of view as to the Court's power and jurisdiction has been a gradual growth. It is highly doubtful whether, one hundred and twenty years ago, the Court would have believed it possible to apply its function to certain classes of controversies which it now determines without any hesitation.

Ninety years ago, there was a grave question whether it would decide a boundary dispute which involved only sovereignty and not property rights of a State. Forty years ago, it was seriously controverted that it could decide a State's liability on its State bonds. Twenty-three years ago, the Court itself was doubtful whether it could take cognizance of State action directed against commerce with another State. Yet all these questions are now recognized as clearly within the Court's jurisdiction. New economic and social conditions have given rise to new sources of controversy; but in each instance, the Court has held itself to be possessed of adequate power to settle them. This has been well expressed by Ex-President Taft as follows: "With the opening up of the country, the conversion of the wilderness of the prairie into industrial and commercial centres, differences of opinion resulting in controversy appeared and found their way to the Supreme Court because of the confidence which its decisions has al-

ready inspired in matters of boundary. It was the
desire for markets beyond its confines which caused
Louisiana to file its bill against the State of Texas;
it was the concern of Missouri for the health of its
people that led it to summon Illinois as a defendant before the Court, lest the waters of the Mississippi should be polluted by that State; it was the
insistence on the part of Kansas that the waters of
the Arkansas, rising in Colorado and flowing through
Kansas, should not be diminished and its people deprived of their accustomed use; and it was an attempt to compel a State of the more perfect Union
to live up to its obligations which justified South
Dakota in appearing aginst North Carolina. The
Supreme Court had broadened its jurisdiction, or
rather, resort was made to a portion thereof untried
if not unsuspected, because the interests of the people, and therefore of the States, were broadening,
and the Supreme Court was seen to be an institution
calculated to meet and to satisfy those needs when
they resulted in controversy between the States."

The history of the Court's gradual but steady
inclusion of additional classes of controversies as
being within its power to adjudicate affords an interesting thought, therefore, in connection with possibilities of judicial settlement between nations.

It is often asserted that there are certain questions
which arise between nations which are *not* suscepti-

ble of arbitration or of submission to a Court—
questions that are purely political, affecting a nation's independence, self-preservation, or domestic
and dynastic policies, which every nation must settle
for itself—situations arising where there may exist
"a deep chasm between conflicting convictions as to
fundamental questions of right, or of national existence or policy," or even between conflicting sentiments or sympathies, deep-seated though irrational,
which may not be bridged by a judicial tribunal.

Yet no jurist or statesman has ever yet found a
touchstone by which it may be infallibly determined
whether any given dispute falls within such category of "non-justiciable" questions.

The old standard was to regard as non-capable of
judicial settlement any question involving "national
honor or vital interest"—so called.[62] But this phrase,
in practical application, was meaningless. The Taft-
Knox arbitration treaties of 1911 (which were
amended to death in the Senate) adopted the word
"justiciable" to signify questions which were capable
of arbitral or judicial decision.[63] The treaties themselves, however, rendered this word also meaningless, by defining it in terms of itself. Thus, the
treaties provided that there should be submitted to
arbitration those controversies "which are justiciable
in their nature, by reason of being susceptible of

decision by the application of the principles of law or equity." But it will be seen that this phraseology did not solve the problem, for it still left vague and undetermined *what subjects are* "susceptible of decision by the application of the principles of law or equity." In other words, the treaty simply said that a "justiciable" controversy should be one which is "justiciable"—a solemn and rather futile piece of tautology reminding one of Pope's famous lines:

> Let observation with extensive view
> Survey mankind from China to Peru.

which some one has said only meant: "Let observation with extensive observation, observe mankind extensively." "What does it all mean?" asked Janicot in Cabell's recent book *The High Place*. "I do not imagine that it means anything," said Florian doubtfully. "It is but an especially dignified manner of saying that I do not care to follow the line of thought you suggest, because logic here might lead to uncomfortable conclusions."

The intricate nature of the attempted distinction has been still further illuminated by an able Princeton professor, who has pointed out that there are "many disputes primarily justiciable in character, that is to say, having a 'legal core' rendering them proper for decision by a Court of justice; but which at the same time unquestionably involve grave political considerations."[64]

Yet in spite of the difficulty—nay, the practical impossibility—of arriving at a definite classification of what questions between nations are or are not "justiciable," the lesson contained in our historical experience with the power of the Supreme Court over State controversies, under the Constitution, may well lead to the following encouraging thought. Just as the development of political, social and economic conditions has, from time to time, convinced the Supreme Court that it was possible to settle judicially subjects which, in earlier days, it considered as incapable of judicial settlement, so it may well happen that nations also will discover that controversies, now deemed by them "nonjusticiable," may, in reality, under changing world conditions, be submitted and practicable for submission to a judicial tribunal. It should never be forgotten that Lord John Russell, during the Civil War, informed the American Ambassador that the Alabama Claims were a subject that affected the "national honor" of Her Majesty's government and could not be arbitrated; yet, nine years later, they *were* so arbitrated, much to the enhancement of British "national honor," even though in defeat of her contentions.

There are, moreover, classes of subjects which are

even now on the borderline between the purely political and domestic, and the strictly international; and changes in world relations, changes in international viewpoints, changes in economic and political conditions, may easily transfer some controversies from the one class to the other. Changes in the standards of law itself may convert "non-justiciable" cases into "justiciable."[65] As instances of a gradual change in international standards and viewpoints, there may be noted the increasing recognition among nations that maltreatment of minority populations in one State may be, to some extent, the concern of another State; that domestic upheavals and internal policies of one State which directly affect the interests or security of another State cannot be wholly regarded as matters of international indifference; that the use of force, within another State, not for the purpose of conquest but for temporary policing— "constabulary use," as it has been called—may be acquiring a certain degree of international recognition. Is it not true too, that the world is slowly but unquestionably awakening to a recognition of the truth of Elihu Root's statement that "violations of the law, of such a character as to threaten the peace and order of the community, of nations, must be deemed to be a violation of the right of every civilized nation to have the law maintained and a legal injury to every nation"?[66]

But the lesson of our experience with the Supreme Court goes still further. Since it is practically impossible for nations to classify and prescribe, in advance, what sources of controversies are and what are not "justiciable," in the narrow sense of that word, what good reason can be advanced why nations should not agree to submit controversies to the compulsory jurisdiction of a Court and to leave it to that Court to decide whether or not the controversy is such as may be settled by the application of principles of law, justice, or equity? The Supreme Court may hold a dispute not to be so determinable (although it has not yet done so). Compulsory submission to a Court to decide, even though the Court might, in the end, hold the cause incapable of judicial decision, would afford a breathing-space, during which the exact facts as to the controversy would be ascertained and made plain to the people of both nations.

Besides the increase in the classes of disputes submitted for the decision of the Supreme Court, one other notable feature in its history is the steady growth in the number of disputes brought by the States before that tribunal. In its first decade, there was one case; in the next sixty years prior to the Civil War, there were seven cases; between 1870 and 1900, there were nine cases; but between 1900 and 1923, there were twenty-two. The American

States have increasingly realized the value of the jurisdiction conferred by the Constitution, and have acquired, it may be said, the habit of resorting to judicial settlement. Like private individuals, States may frequently find that, by staying at home and abusing each other, or by exchanging diplomatic notes, they settle nothing except the more fixed conviction in each of its own self-righteousness. At a distance, each presents a monstrous aspect to the other. Whereas, if they can be brought to meet, face to face, before an impartial tribunal, ill-founded suspicions or convictions may be softened or dissipated. It is a familiar experience to lawyers that clients who swear that they will die rather than settle, often meet before a benign judge, only to find it entirely possible to litigate without acerbity and to accept a decision without enmity. To quote again from the classics: " 'I always thought they (children) were fabulous monsters,' said the Unicorn . . . Alice could not help her lips curling up into a smile, as she began, 'Do you know, I always thought unicorns were fabulous monsters, too.' 'Well, now that we have seen each other,' said the Unicorn, 'if you will believe in me, I'll believe in you. Is that a bargain?' "

An Englishman who has recently written an able book on *The American Supreme Court as an International Tribunal* has well said: "The real value of good Courts is that they develop the habit of peaceful settlement at the expense of fighting. Even in the most violent communities, tribunals that command the public respect will gradually draw to themselves an increasing number of disputes which would otherwise be settled by the use of firearms. All men are largely creatures of habit, and if the method of judicial settlement once comes to be regarded as normal, it will gradually supersede, even though it may never entirely eradicate, the settlement of disputes by violent means. As (Sir Henry) Maine has pointed out, this is exactly what has happened in British India. The establishment of a system of honest and efficient tribunals has drawn to the bar a vast number of disputes which would otherwise have been settled by private vengeance. . . . States are communities of men with the characteristics of men, and statesmen develop habits of government."[67]

The increase in the number of State disputes submitted to the Supreme Court has, without doubt, been due, partly to the growth of popular trust in the wisdom and impartiality of the judges, and partly to the increasing conviction of the complete independence of political considerations shown by the Judges, as proven by the course of the Court's history, and made possible by their permanence of tenure of office.[68]

It will be recalled that one of the sources of weakness of the Courts provided for under the Articles of Confederation of 1781 was that these tribunals were only temporary, appointed specially for each case as it arose, and named from lists of men suggested as Judges by each of the litigant States. The Courts so chosen could not command the entire confidence of the States. The same condition has long impaired a general resort to arbitral tribunals by sovereign nations. The difficulty has always lain in the selection of temporary arbitrators in whose impartiality and ability both parties would have confidence.[69]

When a permanent Court is established, however, consisting of Judges of long tenure, who gradually become entirely disassociated from the active interests and politics of their States or countries, and who, through the process of determining over a long period of years a series of inter-State or international disputes, acquire what has been termed "an international mind," the question presents itself: May there not arise among nations a growth of confidence and a willingness to submit controversies to judicial decision, such as has taken place among the American States in connection with the Supreme Court?

The increase in the number of cases brought before the Supreme Court has also undoubtedly been partly due to the growing realization that there is in existence a body of law which can be properly applied by a Court to disputes between sovereign

States. Thus, it has been found in many cases that the Court did not apply the law of either of the disputing States or the English common law; but that, on the other hand, it specifically stated that the doctrines on which it based its decisions were those of international law or those of civil law writers of continental Europe.[70]

There are, moreover, certain fundamental rules of justice not formulated as doctrines of international law, yet applicable to nations—similar to the concept of the right of an individual not to be deprived of life, liberty and property without due process of law, or similar to the doctrine of title by prescription—which fundamental rules of justice a nation is entitled to insist on as against another nation.[71] As the Supreme Court has held that there are certain "natural rights," belonging to inhabitants of our colonial possessions, of which neither Congress nor the treaty power can deprive them, so, as between inhabitants of different nations, there may be "natural rights" which may furnish a standard for judgment of a Court in case of infringement. Judge Baldwin said long ago: "The submission by the sovereigns or States to a court of law or equity of a controversy between them, without prescribing any rule of decision, gives power to decide according to the appropriate law of the case; which depends on the subject matter, the source and nature of the

[66]

claims of the parties, and the law which governs them. From the time of such submission, the question ceases to be a political one to be decided by the *sic volo, sic jubeo* of political power; it comes to the Court to be decided by its judgment, legal discretion, and solemn consideration of the rules of law appropriate to its nature on a judicial question depending on the exercise of judicial power." Thus, in the Kansas-Colorado Case, the Court took a position midway between the claim of the former State based on the common law, and that of Colorado based on international law, and held that "equality of right and balance of benefits" should be the applicable rule, so far as practicable.

A study of the broad scope of principles by which the Supreme Court has been guided in its judicial decisions ought to strengthen a belief in Americans that there are legal and equitable standards by which, in most instances, controversies between nations could be determined by a Court. This statement, however, does not imply that there exist principles of decision which are now entirely ample and adequate for *every* controversy. Undoubtedly, for the proper performance of its duties by any international Court, and even by the Supreme Court, great assistance would be afforded if the present rules of international law should be reconsidered, restated, or remodelled by some international conference or conferences, so far as the nations can agree upon principles which are applicable to modern conditions, rather than to the conditions of the eighteenth and nineteenth centuries. It must be admitted that, to some extent, a Court at present is hampered by the rigidity, the inelasticity, and the antiquity of many of the existing rules of international law. Unlike the common law, which is moulded by Courts to meet new social and economic conditions as they arise and hence is ever becoming reasonably up to date, international law, arising out of the consent or agreement of nations, has in many directions outlived conditions; it has not kept pace with the development of world relations; and there is always danger in the application of a law, clearly applicable but outworn, based on obsolete conditions suitable to other times and circumstances.[72] Concomitant with the development of judicial tribunals for the settlement of disputes between nations, there must be formulated a modernized statement of international rights and duties, so far as it can be agreed upon by the nations.

IV

INTER-STATE COMPACTS AND
ENFORCEMENT OF DECREES

THE mere fact of the existence of the Court, with its mighty jurisdiction, has not only encouraged a habit on the part of the States of resorting to it for a decision of their controversies, but it has also encouraged an equally important habit of settling such controversies out of Court, by means of compacts entered into between States. The Constitution, while forbidding a State to "enter into an agreement or compact with another State" without the consent of Congress, yet permits such compacts provided Congress gives its assent. It is an interesting fact to note that the increase in the number of suits brought by States has been attended by an equally great increase in the number of such compacts entered into between States. Thus, prior to 1880, there were eleven suits and eight compacts; since 1880, there have been twenty-eight suits and twenty-four compacts. (See Appendix E.)

To the development of this feature of interstate relations under the Constitution, insufficient attention has hitherto been paid by the writers, the statesmen, and the people of this country; and there has been little realization of the meaning of this devel-

opment or of the immense possibilities lying dormant
in this clause of the Constitution. While many of
these thirty-two compacts were concerned with settlement of boundaries, many others dealt with
matters of even greater significance and import; for
they dealt with instances in which the States concerned were willing to surrender a rigid insistence
on their rights and powers of sovereignty, in order to
attain some mutually desirable end. Just as, for the
common peace and welfare, the thirteen, sovereign,
independent States, in 1787, were willing to relinquish the sovereign right of immunity from suit, so
the American States have, in the succeeding years,
found it feasible and desirable, by means of compact, to relinquish the exercise of other sovereign
rights. Here again, the bogy of State sovereignty
and derogation from State honor has not been allowed to stand in the way of mutual benefits.

No sovereign right is more inherent in a state than
that of exclusive control of persons within its own
territory. It is interesting to note, therefore, that
many of these compacts are concerned with the surrender of such exclusive control. Thus, for mutual
convenience, States have agreed that, though their
boundary lines ran through the middle of a river or
its channels, nevertheless, each State should have the
power to serve criminal or civil process on, and to
arrest persons who might actually be outside its own

territory and on, the waters subject to the jurisdiction of the other. In some cases, such arrest has been allowed only for crime committed on the river itself; but in other cases it has been allowed for crimes committed anywhere in the State whose officers make the arrest. In some compacts, these rights to arrest and to serve process have been given to a State, even where the river constituting the boundary line lay wholly within the jurisdiction and territory of the other State.[73] Congress has also authorized the States of Wisconsin, Illinois, Indiana and Michigan to enter into compacts to settle the jurisdiction to be exercised by each State over offences arising out of the claim of either State upon the waters of Lake Michigan.

Such compacts not only represent a striking example of the surrender of a State's exclusive territorial jurisdiction and of the vesting in two independent sovereignties of concurrent power over the same soil, but they also afford interesting occasions for surmise as to the possibility of further surrender of the exercise of sovereign power, through compact. For if one State may agree to allow another to arrest law-breakers and to serve civil and criminal process within its territory, it may, if occasion presents the necessity, allow another State to exercise other sovereign rights within its territory. Thus, one State might allow another State to improve or restrict river navigation, or to exercise sovereign powers over property owned and located within the territory of the first. One State might even allow another to exercise the power of eminent domain in respect to property located within the territory of the first, as, in fact, was done only two years ago, when Kansas and Missouri, each, granted to a city the power to take by eminent domain property located in the other State.

Such compacts might, therefore, vitally modify the relations and rights of the States; and possible developments in this direction are well worthy of the serious thought of American statesmen as well as of international jurists. By such compacts, the authority over certain domestic affairs of one State— part of the police power—a power which the States have never surrendered to the National Government and which they do not desire to so surrender, may be yielded by one State to another, if it shall be deemed to tend to peace and mutual benefit.

The possible improvement of commercial and economic relations between the States, by means of a compact as to legislation, is also a matter for grave consideration. Such compacts might avert the friction now arising between the States over the subject of double, triple, and even more complex taxation, especially in the matter of inheritance taxes, automobile taxes and the like. The suppression of spread of disease, infection, and noxious things of all kinds may be a very proper subject of compact.

It is announced in the newspapers that the great dispute between Colorado and Kansas, between the irrigation ditch owners of the one State and the farmers of the other, is now (after long years of Court litigation) about to be settled by compact. The still more excited dispute between the sovereign States of Arizona, California, Colorado, Nevada, New Mexico, Utah and Wyoming as to the equitable apportionment of the waters of the great Colorado River and its tributaries, is now in process of settlement by a seven-party, State compact—such compact regulating not merely the flow of the river in each State but also providing for the building of reservoirs in some States for the benefit of other States. Minnesota, North Dakota and South Dakota were given assent by Congress, in 1917, to make compacts for improvement of navigation and control of floods on boundary waters and tributaries—North Dakota having sued Minnesota for damages occasioned by alleged acts of the latter State in flooding the farms of the former States.

The control and development of the great commercial interests of New York and New Jersey, involving all the cities using the waters of New York Harbor, are now being regulated by means of compacts between the two States under which one great port is to be constituted as to the terminal and transportation facilities for these cities, and erecting a new "body corporate and politic" termed the Port of New York District, with commissioners chosen by each State, to administer it. Another recent compact between New York and New Jersey has regulated tunnels under the waters between them, and the fixing of tolls therein. By a recent compact between Missouri and Kansas (before referred to) each State relinquishes its right to tax property in it, belonging to a waterworks system which serves jointly two cities located in the respective States.

One of the most interesting examples of the possibilities lying within this compact clause of the Constitution is the National Forest Conservation Act of 1911, under which Congress gave a blanket permission and consent "to each of the several States of the Union to enter into any agreement . . . with any other State or States for the purpose of conserving the forests and the water supply of the States entering into such agreement or compact."

Still another interesting possibility lies in the recent proposal by Governor Pinchot of Pennsylvania that a solution for the anthracite coal problem be arrived at by compact between all the States using such coal—such compact being necessary, since the Federal Government has apparently no power over coal mining, that business not being interstate commerce, and since no one State can regulate all the various features of the coal problem—extending from production to marketing. Thus, such a compact would represent a great advance into a new field of government in this country—the introduction of a capacity for regulation, midway between the Federal power and the State power—the exercise by *several* States of a power, which could not, as a practical matter, be exercised by *one* State alone, and which could not be exercised by Congress at all, in view of its restricted authority under the Constitution.

While the Supreme Court has never definitely construed the meaning of the words "agreement or compact," there have been intimations in some cases to the effect that only political compacts or agreements which affected the sovereignty of the States as between themselves or as between them and the National Government were sought to be regulated or controlled by this clause in the Constitution, i.e., agreements which increase the political powers of a State or encroach on the national dominion.[74] It is unnecessary to consider the question in detail; for certainly any compact of serious importance enough to raise any State controversy would be regarded as political and requiring Congressional assent.

The development of these interstate compacts is noteworthy for two reasons, in particular. First,

they present significant instances of the voluntary
surrender or restriction by States of the exercise of
other sovereign rights or powers than that of immunity from suit. Second, they show that the Supreme Court may now at any time be confronted with
a new class of controversies between States, namely
those due to breaches of such compacts. In case of
the violation of its compact by a State, the interesting
question will arise: to what extent may the Court
intervene to enforce the compact ?[75] Should the compact require State action of a political nature, how
far can the Court go in decreeing the performance of
such action? It is undoubtedly true that there are
certain political acts which no Court can require a
State to do. This fact, however, constitutes no argument against the Court's power to determine what
the rights of the parties are; for even in suits on
contracts between private individuals, there are
many affirmative actions one party may have con-
tracted to perform, but which a Court has no power
to decree shall be done.

The question of the extent to which a violation of
a compact between States can be adjusted by decision
of the Supreme Court, naturally leads us to a consideration of the great question which is always presented when the subject of settlement of any international dispute by peaceful tribunals is discussed—
the question: how is the tribunal's decision to be en-

forced? And it is often said that, in the capability of enforcement, there lies a distinction between decision of controversies of American States and decision of differences between wholly independent nations. That there may be such a distinction must be admitted; and yet our history will show that it is not so great, and that it does not constitute so conclusive an argument, as may, at first thought, appear.

There is one very prevalent mistake about the Supreme Court and the enforcement of its judgments and decrees. The Court does not enforce them. That duty ultimately lies on the Executive, through the medium of such inherent powers as he possesses and of such statutory means as Congress may provide. When the Constitution says that the President is to "take care that the laws are faithfully executed," it includes within the word "laws," not only statute laws but decisions of the highest Court. As early as 1792, Congress authorized the President to call forth the militia "to execute the laws of the Union, and suppress insurrections"; and when the Governor of Pennsylvania, in 1809, asked President Madison to intervene against a decree of the Supreme Court, Madison replied: "The Executive is not only unauthorized to prevent the execution of a decree sanctioned by the Supreme Court of the United States, but is especially enjoined by statute to carry into effect any such decree, where opposition may be made to it." The Marshal of the Court, who serves the Court's writ of execution and enforces its judgment in the first instance, is an Executive officer, even though acting, to some extent, under direction of the Court. The writ itself is issued in the name of the United States of America and of the President of the United States, and not in the name of the Court.[76] It is an error, therefore, to speak of the Court as enforcing its decrees. It delivers its judgment and issues its mandate and other judicial process, and there its judicial powers end. In case of disobedience by the loser in the suit, the responsibility for ultimate enforcement lies elsewhere than on the Court.

Though the question whether the judgment of the Supreme Court, as between States, could ever be carried into effectual execution was raised at the very outset, in 1793, it is a singular fact that this question was not definitely settled until one hundred and twenty-five years later.[77]

In the year 1918, the question was directly raised in the famous case of *Virginia* v. *West Virginia*. After prolonged litigation, and exhaustive consideration by the Court, the State of Virginia had finally obtained a decree for the payment by West Virginia of over $12,000,000, with interest at five per cent, as the share of Virginia's pre-war debt due from West Virginia. Since the latter State made no move for payment, Virginia asked to Court to issue a writ of execution; and the Court refused its issue until after the Legislature of West Virginia should meet and be given "a reasonable opportunity to provide for payment of the judgment." The West Virginia Legislature failing to make such provision, the Court, on a renewed motion by Virginia for a writ, unanimously held that its right to pronounce a judgment necessarily implied, under the Constitution, the right in the Court and the President to use the appropriate means or such means as are at its or his disposal for enforcement of the judgment against the State and its governmental agencies; and it unequivocally decided that power exists in Congress to provide for the execution of the Court's judgment. The Court left open for subsequent argument before it the question of how far, under existing legislation of Congress, it possessed the power to issue a process that would be adequate or capable of securing the fulfillment of the judgment by West Virginia. No further argument was ever had on these points, as the State of West Virginia finally yielded and entered into an agreement with Virginia for the payment of the judgment rendered against it.[78]

In considering whether a judicial decree can be carried into execution against an American State, it must be noted that, in inter-State cases, there are three different types of relief which the complaining State may ask of the Court. First, it may seek a judgment putting it in possession of disputed territory. Ordinarily, such a judgment would execute itself. But even if officers of the losing State should oppose its execution, there are judicial remedies open; for the offending State officers, as individuals, could themselves be sued civilly or indicted criminally in the Federal Courts. Second, a State may ask for an injunction to restrain another State from committing certain alleged unlawful acts. An injunction, if disobeyed by State officials, may be enforced by civil or criminal proceedings against such officials as individuals. Third, a State may ask for some affirmative action by the Court, requiring the other State as a State and in its governmental capacity, to do some act—for instance it may ask the Court to issue a mandamus to a State Governor or members of the Legislature, as Virginia did in the West Virginia case. The Supreme Court has never yet decided how far it can go in this direction,[79] but it has clearly stated that there is no doubt that Congress has the power to authorize adequate forms of procedure.

But in all three classes of cases, the State officials who refused to obey would be subject, as individuals, to civil and criminal proceedings in the Federal Courts. It thus appears that, under the American form of government, enforcement of decrees against States may be largely obtained, through enforcement of personal liability of State officials for disobedience to the Court and for violation of criminal or other laws enacted by Congress for the purpose of executing the Court's orders.

This principle of individual liability, in cases of failure of a State to comply with the decrees of the Court, raises an interesting question as to the possibility of future development of the same principle, in cases of a breach by a nation of the rules of international law. Of course, its application would have a very limited field, owing to the fact that, as a rule, actions violative of international law, or other actions leading to war, are generally committed by officials in pursuance of express instruction from the Government of the nation. War may result, however, from *unauthorized* actions of individuals or officials, actions which, under present standards of so-called national honor, a nation may feel called upon to adopt as its own. Is it not possible that nations might by treaty agree, in advance, that, for actions of this kind committed in time of peace, there should be trial before an international tribunal and the imposition of damages or other penalty in case of conviction? Why should not such actions be submitted to the calming influence of judicial determination, rather than allowed to become a possible *casus belli* by reason of hasty adoption by the nation as a national act, in the heat of the moment? Why should not such an action as the recent firing upon Corfu after one hour's notice be the subject of judicial investigation, even assuming that the occupation of Corfu itself was a lawful act (a very extreme assumption, be it said).

The principal of individual liability for illegal actions in time of war has received an interesting application, only a year ago, in the Treaty in relation to the Use of Submarines and Noxious Gases in Warfare, signed by the five Powers, February 6, 1922, which by Article III, provides as follows:

The Signatory Powers, desiring to insure the enforcement of the humane rules of existing law declared by them with respect to attacks upon and the seizure and destruction of merchant ships, further declare that any person in the service of any Power who shall violate any of those rules, whether or not such person is under orders of a governmental superior, shall be deemed to have violated the laws of war and shall be liable to trial and punishment as if for an act of piracy and may be brought to trial before the civil or military authorities of any Power within the jurisdiction of which he may be found.

Here is a clear and effective imposition of individual liability for a violation of an international law. The Versailles Treaty and the Treaty with Austria contain a somewhat similar recognition of the principle, by which Germany and Austria recognize "the right of the Allied and Associated Powers to bring before military tribunals persons accused of having committed acts in violation of the laws and customs of war."

But individual liability for violations of law in time of war can never be made effective, so long as the unqualified doctrine prevails that a subordinate is not responsible for what he does under orders of his superiors.[80] Such a doctrine has no place in American constitutional law; for in this country, neither the authority of a superior officer, if in violation of a law, nor the authority of law if in violation of the Constitution, will save a man from liability. The question may well be discussed whether the doctrine should have any place in international law or in the law of war. While it may be urged that, in time of war, there are differences in conditions and in reasons for the existence of the defence that an act was committed under orders, it is clear that the whole subject deserves careful reconsideration by nations desirous of the observance of international law, both in peace and war. At all events, so far as this country is concerned, before we are required to fall back on the element of force for the execution of a Court's judgment against a State, we have this element of individual liability.

There is one other factor of the greatest importance in the settlement of interstate controversies which can be relied upon, before a resort to force—

the factor of Time—that "old common arbitrator Time," to use Shakespeare's words. It is this molli-fier of disputes to whose aid the Supreme Court has often resorted; for as Seneca wrote: "Time hath often cured the wound which reason failed to heal." The angry feelings of individuals can rarely be kept at highest tension for long periods. The same thing is true as to the popular clamors and passions of States. Time, moreover, changes the aspect of what is often falsely termed "national honor." "In troubled times," said James Russell Lowell, "the blood mounts to the head and colors the judgment, giving to suspicions and fancies the force of realities and intensifying personal predilections till they seem the pith and substance of national duties." And William J. Bryan has well phrased this same thought, more colloquially: "When a man is angry, every question is a question of honor, every interest is a vital interest. Man angry is a very different animal from man calm; when a man is angry, he swaggers about and talks about what he can do, and he gener-ally overestimates it; when he is calm, he thinks about what he ought to do and listens to the voice of conscience."

Hence it was, that Secretary of State Knox in his Arbitration Treaties of 1911, and Secretary of State Bryan in his Peace Treaties of 1915, provided that, in case of a dispute between States not susceptible

[84]

of arbitration, neither State would go to war until after the lapse of a period devoted to inquiry into facts by an impartial commission.[81] A chance to cool off is the solution of many differences arising from anger and unreason. An inquiry into facts in 1908, at a time when the public feeling in England was aroused to a high pitch, probably averted a war with Russia—the Dogger Bank episode, when the Russian fleet fired on English fishermen, under the mistaken belief that they were Japanese. And President Schurman has well said: "In the history of civilization, it is not too much to say that the reign of justice has been established by securing an interval between injury and revenge."

Moreover, time gives opportunity to establish the facts. "Time tries the truth in everything," was said long ago. It is chiefly due to ignorance of facts and misunderstanding of words and motives that peoples (as distinguished from their governments) are willing to go to war. Voltaire succinctly noted the difference between "those who peaceably investigate the truth, and those who war for words they do not understand." It may well happen that a war could be avoided if there could not only be an agreement as to what are the facts involved, *but also an agreement as to what the disagreement is about*. A very clear thinker has recently written: "I cannot conceive that anyone will deny that the real causes of important

[85]

modern wars are different from the avowed reasons for them, or that the gaining of popular support for most wars depends upon the power of foreign offices and the press to confuse the two."[82] Though it is often said that modern wars have their source in economic causes, yet few people would be willing to declare war expressly for economic or commercial gain. Oil might be the real cause of a war with Mexico; but the American people would never go to war, with this as the avowed cause; nor would any American Administration admit it to be such.

It is because the real causes are so frequently covered up by a mist of words about national honor and self-preservation, that people believe their own grounds for war to be righteous, and, so believing, frequently enter upon a war, with motives conceived as ethically right and essentially idealistic. Time may be the dispeller of such mists and a revealer of the bald and unethical facts lying concealed. A prescribed breathing space for an investigation of facts, whether by a Commission or a Court, would render it hard to keep up these confusions between real and avowed causes of war.

It will be seen that the Supreme Court has thoroughly realized the emollient influence of the lapse of years; and, while not countenancing unnecessary delays, it has regarded cases between States as susceptible of grave circumspection in the taking of each successive step both by counsel and the Court. Thus the Rhode Island-Massachusetts Case was pending in the Court fourteen years—from 1832 to 1846—with the result that though great excitement attended its initiation, its decision was received by the two States with calm acquiescence. The Alabama-Georgia Case was pending for five years (1855-1860); the Kansas-Colorado Case, for six years (1901-1907); the Missouri-Illinois Case, for seven years (1900-1907); the Maryland-West Virginia Case, for nineteen years (1891-1910); the Virginia-West Virginia Case, for twelve years (1906-1918); the Wyoming-Colorado Case for eleven years (1911-1922); and the Texas-Oklahoma Case is still pending after over four years of litigation (1919-1924). Most of these cases began with hard feelings, and ended with placid and un-vexed acceptance of the decision. Well might the cheerful Mr. Roker remark to Mr. Pickwick: "What a rum thing Time is, ain't it?"

But even where neither Time nor individual lia-bility can bring about the compliance with an execu-tion of the Court's judgment, the application of actual force may not be a necessary alternative for such execution. For history shows that nations and States, alike, are reluctant to appear to the world as law-breakers or as Court-flouters.

In the lapse of one hundred and thirty-four years, no State of the American Union has refused to comply with and obey the decision of the Supreme Court in an inter-State suit. And so far as international arbitral tribunals are concerned, their decisions, while differing from those of Courts of compulsory jurisdiction, are, nevertheless, sometimes quite as unpleasant to the losing party, as those of a Court; yet it has been stated by a well-known international jurist that "since the re-entry of arbitration into the world by the Jay Treaty in 1795, there is really no well-authenticated case of a refusal to abide by a judgment."[83]

John Dryden's famous line—"right lives by law, and law subsists by power"—may have been true in the artificial and unidealistic eighteenth century, but it is not true now. More and more, sentiment, and public sentiment, are replacing force as the basis of the execution of law. Just as domestic statutory laws cannot now rest on force alone, but must have the support of the community belief, so gradually men are coming to realize that international action and international judgments will depend for their permanence on international approval. And, correlatively, if there is a widespread approval by nations of a Court judgment in an international case, the particular States involved will find it increasingly difficult to challenge and flout such approval. This is but another way of stating that what the framers of our Declaration of Independence termed "a decent respect for the opinions of mankind" is becoming a factor in the determination of the relations of nations—a factor which it will be increasingly difficult for contending nations to disregard. The pessimistic think that the experience during and since the Great War is evidence to the contrary. Let them recall, however, how anxiously German scholars and German officials sought to justify to the neutral nations their various breaches of international law. Had even Germany thoroughly believed that her deeds could be justified solely by the rule of force, she would not have sought to convince the world that she was supported by the law. And no nation today is sanguine enough really to believe that it can adopt Birdofredom Sawin's theory:

> Thet our nation's bigger'n theirn,
> An' so its rights air bigger.

Whether we are idealistic, and refer it to evolution, education, Christianity, or humanity; or whether we are realistic, and refer it to the radio, the aeroplane, gasoline, the press, the gunsmith and the chemist—no one can deny today that nations are slowly, very slowly, grasping the fact that they are a community. And in a community, not even the biggest man can say—I will live and do as I please.

In addition, however, to the application of the doctrine of individual liability, the influence of lapse of time, and the pressure of public opinion, there is one other possible influence which may be employed by nations against an offending nation which should violate an agreement or treaty entered into by it or which should refuse to comply with a judicial or arbitral decree. One difficulty with any agreement by nations to employ force of some kind, either military or economic, against a non-complying nation, is that the obligation thus imposed is one which might bear heavily on, and be prejudicial to the nations using such force, themselves. Thus, the employment of, what has been termed, an economic boycott might injure the boycotter nation and its citizens more than it did the boycottee; it might also in practice be extremely difficult of enforcement.

There is, however, one form of pressure which might be used against a non-complying nation, which under certain conditions, would be extremely effective, easy of application, and non-injurious to the nation applying it. This form of pressure would consist *not* in an agreement by nations to *assume an obligation* to act against an offender, but in an agreement to be *relieved of existing obligations* towards such offender.

The outbreak of a war, under present international law, at once brings into operation and imposes on nations which are not parties to the war, heavy and troublesome burdens and rules of action both negative and positive, known as the obligations of neutrals. These obligations, created by international law, have been chiefly of benefit to the belligerents. The question may well be asked: why such benefit should accrue to any belligerent which should indulge in war in violation of law, or of its agreement or of a judicial decree?

Though the suggestion has not been made heretofore, so far as I am aware, may it not be possible that a perfectly practical means of pressure, nonburdensome to the nations exerting it, may be found in the following proposal: that nations should become parties to an agreement whereby, whenever any one of them should violate the agreement or should fail to comply with an international treaty or judicial or arbitral decree, so that war should result, all the non-combatant nations should be relieved of all obligations or duties of neutrality imposed by international law? In other words, that, should X Nation, a party to any such agreement, make war on Y Nation, in violation of the agreement or of a treaty or of an international court decree, all the other parties to the agreement should be relieved from the duty of enforcing their neutrality laws, and should be under no liability therefor to the offending X Nation.

Thus, with such an agreement in force in advance, in case of such a violation by X, the United States and all other non-belligerent nations would auto-

matically cease to be under any duty to prevent en-
listment of troops by the enemy of X or to prevent
the fitting out or supplying war-ships in their ports
by the enemy of X; or to be under duty to forbid the
use of their ports to prize captures by the enemy of
X; or to be under any duty to intern for failure
to leave their ports within twenty-four hours, any
warships or their crews; or to be under any duty
to intern troops entering their territory; or to be
under any duty to prevent the establishment of
radio stations in their territory for use of the enemy
of X in communicating with vessels at sea or with
land forces. Such an agreement made in advance, re-
leasing non-belligerent nations from existing duties,
in the event of a breach of international duty by one
of the parties to the agreement, would certainly not
be objectionable to any one except to the offending
party; for, unlike agreements to employ military or
economic pressure, it would lighten the burdens on
the parties to the agreement, instead of increasing
them.

Should an agreement be entered into by nations
consenting to such release from neutral obligations,
on specified contingencies of violation of its obligations by any of the signatories, then upon the hap-
pening of any such contingency, the failure of a
non-combatant to enforce the laws of neutrality, being a failure permitted by and in accordance with

[92]

such an agreement, could not be regarded as an act of war or as action connoting a taking part in the war, or as directed either in favor of or against any of the parties to the war. It would simply constitute the taking advantage by a non-combatant of a privilege to which it was entitled by agreement signed beforehand by the offending nation. That its effect would undoubtedly be injurious to the latter would be one of the results intended by the agreement, and intended as one of the means of enforcement of international obligations. Moreover, while the possibility of the exercise of such a privilege by non-combatant nations might not prevent war or violation by a nation of its obligations under treaty, agreement, or judicial decree, it might well prove a powerful deterrent to such a violation—just as the possibility of an economic boycott may be a deterrent, as well as a means of punishment. The existence of such a possibility might well influence the course of action of a nation which was calculating the respective advantages of peace or war or the possible gains or losses to ensue from a failure to respect its international obligations.

One who, as Assistant Attorney General of the United States, was charged with the duty from 1914 to 1917 of enforcing the neutrality laws and obligations of this country, can personally testify to the relief which would have been afforded to the United

States, had any such general agreement of nations been in force in 1914, and to the seriousness of the possible results to a nation which had violated its treaties, should such violation have been attended with a release of the other non-combatant nations from all or any of their neutral obligations.

Whether or not these suggestions are practical; whether international questions are or are not susceptible of judicial settlement; whether any present Court can operate as an aid to peace; whether the nations are approaching in any degree towards a willingness to submit to a Court with compulsory jurisdiction—these are all international problems, which citizens of this country will be called upon to confront in the coming years. If any feel pessimistic over the present conditions of the nations of the world, let them take courage by recalling that it is not the first time in history that men see "as in a glass, darkly."

Four thousand years before Christ, some discouraged priest or statesman in Egypt inscribed on a stone these words:[84]

Our earth is degenerate in these latter days. There are signs that the world is coming to an end. Children no longer obey their parents. Everybody wants to write a book. The end of the world is manifestly drawing near.

ENFORCEMENT OF DECREES

Three hundred years ago, in 1646, James Howell wrote to the Earl of Dorset:

And now, my Lord, to take all Nations in a lump, I think God Almighty hath a quarrel lately with all mankind, and hath given the reins to the ill spirit to compass the whole Earth; for within these twelve years, there have been the strangest revolutions, the horridest things happen, not only in Europe, but all the World over, that have befallen mankind, I dare boldly say, since Adam fell, in so short a revolution of time . . . so that it seems the whole Earth is off the hinges.

So, while it may seem that the jealousies and animosities between nations are now at such height as to preclude all idea of judicial settlement of difficulties, let us recall that, in 1787, when the Supreme Court was created, similar jealousies, similar insistence on the preservation of sovereign rights, and similar frictions between the States, raised the gravest doubts in the minds of many sober Americans as to the successful operation of the new form of government then under discussion. And on this phase of the subject, the striking words of a great Princetonian and a great American patriot are pertinent. On February 4, 1890, at the Centennial Celebration of the first session of the Supreme Court, Grover Cleveland said:

[95]

Our fathers had sacrificed much to be free. Above all, they desired freedom to be absolutely secured to themselves and their posterity. And yet, with all their enthusiasm for that sentiment, they were willing to refer to the tribunal which they devised, all questions arising under their newly formed Constitution, affecting the freedom and protection and safety of the citizen. Though bitter experience had taught them that the instrumentalities of government might trespass upon freedom, and they had learned in a hard school the cost of the struggle to wrest liberty from the grasp of power, they refused, in the solemn work they had in hand, to take counsel of undue fear or distracting perturbation, and they calmly and deliberately established as a function of their government a check upon unauthorized freedom and a restraint upon dangerous liberty. Their attachment and allegiance to the sovereignty of their States were warm and unfaltering; but these did not prevent them from contributing a fraction of that sovereignty to the creation of a Court which should guard and protect their new nation, and save and perpetuate a government which should, in all time to come, bless an independent people.

It was a limited surrender or renunciation of certain specific rights and powers of sovereignty by the States, in the interests of peace and harmony and union, that saved the United States. Who can say that it may not require a similar relinquishment of some rights and powers of sovereignty by the nations of the world, to save our modern civilization?

Nations have long insisted on a Bill of Rights. Is it not time that they considered the framing of a Bill of Duties?

And duty and right are not always opposing terms.

Individual men recognize that to help to preserve the peace of the community is not only one of their duties, but one of their rights and privileges. May it not be possible that the same individual men, when banded together as a sovereign State, will also recognize that the same duty and privilege exist to help to preserve the peace of the world community? In the case both of an individual and of a State, the task, undoubtedly, may require a waiver of complete independence of action. Why should not such a waiver be made, if necessary for so great an end? If we cannot believe now that it is possible of accomplishment, let us, at all events, hope it to be possible. Let us retain at least a spark of that flaming confidence expressed in the magnificent words of Jean Paul Richter that: "There will come a time when it shall be light; and when man shall awaken from his lofty dreams, and find his dreams still there, and that nothing has gone save his sleep."

APPENDIX A

Pennsylvania v. Connecticut

The case of *Pennsylvania* v. *Connecticut* was reported in the newspapers at the time, as follows (these extracts never having been since republished).

Freeman's Journal (Phil.) Jan. 23, 1782: "Measures have been taken to settle the claim (of Connecticut). . . . The State of Pennsylvania has summoned her competitors to appear before Congress on the first day of June next by agents duly authorized, in order that Commissioners may be appointed to hear and determine between the joining boundaries of the two States. Thus there is a prospect that all uncertainties concerning the extent of Pennsylvania will be removed before long; especially a commission between the latter and New Jersey will soon meet to form an equal and certain division of the river Delaware, the common highway of both States, in order to take away the gross abuses which have arisen from the pretence that the island in the said river and the land covered by water are without jurisdiction, thus offering a sanctuary for fugitives and criminals."

Ibid., Nov. 17, 1782, stating that a "Court of Commissioners" had met and organized in the Pennsylvania-Connecticut case.

Ibid., Jan. 21, 1783: "On the 18th of November a quorum attended and the commission was read; they were then sworn and the Court was solemnly opened. The Hon. William Whipple having been previously elected president of the Court by ballot.

APPENDIX A

The agents for the respective States then produced their several credentials. The agents for Connecticut then moved that the petition preferred by the Executive Council of Pennsylvania to Congress praying the appointment of the Court should be produced; which, on argument, was overruled. A motion was then made in writing, on the part of Connecticut, that as there were several persons, to the number of 2000, residing on a part of the lands in controversy who had long held and improved the same who would be materially affected by the decision, and who had no legal notice of the appointment of the Court, no farther proceedings should be had until they were duly cited to appear. This was opposed by the agents of Pennsylvania, as calculated merely for delay, and to disappoint the intentions of Congress and the parties. They farther alleged that the case of the settlers was provided for in the Articles of Confederation which gave a further trial upon the private right of soil, in which they would be proper parties. Of this opinion was the Court; and the motion was also overruled. The agents for Pennsylvania by this time clearly perceiving that delay was affected on the part of Connecticut, and apprehending that after the evidence was opened, further attempts of that nature would be made, gave notice in writing that they should oppose any such motion after the testimony had been opened, and the merits of the cause entered into on the part of Pennsylvania; but that if any such motion was to be made, they acquiesced in giving time for that purpose. To this, the agents for Connecticut replied in substance, that as Pennsylvania had filed no declaration or state of her claim, and knowing that there were many proofs and exhibits on their part, which were necessary to the cause, particularly sundry enumerated Indian deeds which had been left in England, and not knowing what concessions might be made on the part of Pennsylvania, they consented to proceed in the cause, reserving to themselves, and allowing also to Pennsylvania, the right of moving an adjournment in any stage of the cause, as the nature and exigence of the case might require. To this, the agents for Pennsylvania replied that they were ready and had been for some time to exhibit their claim, but had delayed it, on the promise made by Connecticut to file their claim at the same time; that as to the right of postponing the cause at any time, they could not agree to any such motion after the trial on the merits had begun; and prayed the opinion of the Court. Upon consideration of the motion, the Court was of opinion it was premature; that the cause should go on, and either party might move an adjournment, of which the Court would judge on the circumstance and merits. The Attorney General of Pennsylvania then in a masterly address opened the cause on its merits on the part of his State. After passing some just and elegant encomiums on the Constitution of the Court, as founded in reason, justice and benevolence to mankind, he went into the particulars of the title of Pennsylvania."

Pennsylvania Packet, Dec. 17, 1782: "It is expected that the counsel in the great cause between Connecticut and Pennsylvania now debating before the Commissioners authorized by Congress at Trenton will be fully heard before the end of this week."

APPENDIX A

Pennsylvania Packet, Dec. 28, 1782: "They write from Trenton that on Tuesday last (Dec. 24) the argument before the Court sitting there on the great controversy between Connecticut and Pennsylvania was conducted by Joseph Reed, Esquire, counsel for the latter. The judges have the matter under consideration and it is supposed they may decide upon it next week."

Pennsylvania Packet, Jan. 2, 1783: "We are authorized to assure the public that the dispute which has so long depended between this State and the State of Connecticut is finally determined in favour of Pennsylvania. The Commissioners appointed by the parties, under the sanction of Congress agreeably to the ninth article of the Confederation, passed sentence unanimously in our favour on Monday last" (Dec. 30, 1782).

Freeman's Journal, Jan. 8, 1783: "The cause lately decided between the State and Connecticut must be highly interesting to the United States as well as those who are the immediate parties. Some of the principles affect the extensive claims of several of the States. A short view of the dispute must therefore be acceptable, not only to these, but even to a speculative reader. The printer, therefore, will from good authority, present his readers in some succeeding papers with a short abstract of the most material particulars of this important cause."

Freeman's Journal, Jan. 29, Feb. 5, 1783, set forth in detail the legal points made by the agents of each State in behalf of their respective States.

Independent Chronicle (Boston), Jan. 13, 20, 27,

APPENDIX A

Feb. 3, 10, 17, March 17, 1785, reprinting from the *Connecticut Courant* detailed articles on the claim of Connecticut and the proceedings of the Court, in which the following interesting comments appeared:

(Feb. 3, 1785.) "The conduct of that high Court at Trenton stands without a precedent in the record of judicial proceedings. To enter into a previous agreement not to publish the grounds of their opinions—to resolve that the opinion of the majority should be denominated unanimous, are such singular, unprecedented proceedings as to raise in the minds of impartial men the most violent suspicions of the integrity of their views. These suspicions are strongly confirmed by the declaration of some of the Commissioners who avow their dissatisfaction with the decision. Two honest men out of five is a very great proportion in the world at large; that it is a greater proportion than Pennsylvania can produce in the controversy, I believe the public will be convinced when they have read the transactions of the State subsequent to the decree at Trenton. . . .

"Certain instances respecting this decree are very singular. It was previously resolved by the Commissioners that the opinion of the majority should be determined unanimous and that their several opinions and the reasons on which they were built should be kept private. Accordingly, we find the decree is very concise, not supported by any public reasons, and called unanimous, though we are credibly informed that two of the five Commissioners were in favour of Connecticut. We likewise have it from good authority that a very respectable member of Congress, upon hearing the proceedings of the Court

[103]

and decree in favour of Pennsylvania, exclaimed, 'God bless me! How could they give such a decision when the stating on the part of Pennsylvania, is sufficient to turn the question against her?' We have likewise good authority to assert that some material evidence in favour of Connecticut was suppressed, having unluckily fallen into the hands of some gentleman in Pennsylvania, interested in the controverted lands. . . . In short, the whole proceedings of the State of Pennsylvania from the beginning of the controversy to the present time appear to be the united efforts of force and dishonesty."

(March 17, 1785.) "Connecticut has suffered a very great injury in her charter rights by the decision of the high Court at Trenton. But the decree is final and Connecticut must acquiesce, unless it can be proved that there was some misconduct in the proceedings. . . . To adjust all the contending interests of the several States is a task worthy of the most careful attention of the Supreme Council of America."

APPENDIX B

RATIFICATION OF THE CONSTITUTION

Marshall, C. J., said in *McCulloch* v. *Maryland* (1819), 4 Wheaton 316, 403: "No political dreamer was ever wild enough to think of breaking down the lines which separate the States, and of compounding the American people into one common mass. Of consequence, when they act, they act in their States."

The fact set forth by Madison has been beclouded by the political necessities which have led most American statesmen and historians, especially of the North, to attempt to make history conform to their view of national sovereignty. As Albion W. Small well said in *The Beginnings of American Nationality* (1890): "The facts of American History were very early confounded with the definitions and doctrines of a dogmatic political philosophy. Before our Constitution was three score years old, it had been associated with a mass of theoretical and fanciful folk lore, whose authenticity was more vehemently asserted than were the facts themselves. A body of tradition grew up about the origins of our nationality, and it became the mould in which all conclusions from documentary sources must be cast. This apocryphal element obscured the genuine portions of our history, and became the criterion by which events were judged, instead of remaining an hypothesis which the examination of evidence should justify or destroy. The general view of our national development, which found its ablest political champion in Daniel Webster, discovered in the history of the

United States an experience absolutely unprecedented. It saw a nation 'born in a day.' It saw, nevertheless, the anomalous spectacle of repeatedly
threatened and finally attempted self-destruction, in
the body thus spontaneously generated. Persons who
have approached the study, since the interpretation
of our Constitution ceased to be a subject for angry
dispute, are to be pardoned if they suspect that the
point of observation from which our history presents
such a phenomenal aspect was not fortunately
chosen. It is not surprising that men who have been
taught to trace between all historical causes and ef-
fects the slow procession of gradual advance, are
suspicious of the alleged singular exception."

In the 1830's, Daniel Webster and Judge Story, in
their effort to repel the insidious doctrine of Nullification, advanced the theory that the Constitution
was adopted by the people of the Union as a whole,
and contended that this was the meaning of the
preamble: "We, the People of the United States."
This doctrine, later maintained by Northern statesmen down to and through the Civil War, served a
notable political purpose in centering men's attention on the Union; but it, in fact, had no historical
basis. *Story on the Constitution*, I, Sections 363, 352;
see also Wilson, J., and Jay, C. J., in *Chisholm* v.
Georgia (1793), 4 Dallas 419.

Practically the only men of eminence among the
framers of the Constitution who took this extreme
Nationalistic position were James Wilson of Pennsylvania, and Alexander Hamilton of New York.
Their views, however, were not an index of the general sentiment of their time. The great bulk of those

who favored adoption of the Constitution knew and insisted upon the fact that it was the sovereign people of each separate State, which ratified the great instrument, through delegates chosen by the people to act for them in State Conventions called by the State Legislatures. That there was no difference as to the sovereignty which ratified the Articles of Confederation and the Constitution is to be seen from the phraseology of the ratifications by Massachusetts. The former, on March 10, 1778, was:

"We, therefore, the Council and House of Representatives of this State in General Court assembled do, *in the name and behalf of the good people of this State*, instruct you, their Delegates, to subscribe such Articles of Confederation and Perpetual Union which were recommended by Congress."

The latter on February 6, 1788, was:

"The Convention . . . do, *in the name and behalf of the People of the Commonwealth of Massachusetts*, assent to and ratify the said Constitution for the United States of America."

The agents differed, being in once case the Legislature, in the other the Convention; but in each case the agents acted for the same principal. See especially *The Motley Letter*, by Henry B. Dawson, *The Historical Magazine* (July 5, 1861), X.

When Webster cited the wording of the preamble, "We, the People of the United States," he was ignorant of the manner in which these words were inserted in the draft of the Constitution; for Madison's *Notes of the Debates on the Federal Convention* had not been published when Webster spoke, and the historic facts as to these debates were unknown. When the draft of the preamble was first submitted on August 6, 1787, by John Rutledge for the Committee of Detail, it read: "We, the people of the States, New Hampshire, Massachusetts," etc. (enumerating each of the thirteen States) "do ordain and establish this Constitution for the Government of ourselves and posterity." It was so adopted unanimously by the Convention. On September 8, a Committee was appointed to revise the style and arrange the articles already assented to by the Convention; and on September 12, this Committee reported the final draft of the Constitution, in which the preamble was changed to read as it now appears. But neither this Committee nor any one else in the Convention assumed that it was changing the substantive meaning of the preamble and articles previously agreed upon. The reason for the change was plain. Article VII of the draft provided that the Constitution should become effective, "between the States so ratifying the same" upon ratification by nine States. No one could tell which or how many of the thirteen States would ratify. It was impossible, therefore, to name specifically (as the first draft did) each and all the States, as establishing this Constitution, since some of the States so recited might not ratify the instruments as so drawn. Hence, instead of the wording, "We, the people of New Hampshire, Massachusetts," etc., there was adopted the wording, "We, the people of the United States," the word "United States" meaning the people of those States who should unite,

APPENDIX B

through ratifying the instrument. *James Madison's Notes of Debates* (1918) by James Brown Scott, 84-87. See also *Studies in the History of the Federal Convention of 1787*, by John F. Jameson, *Amer. Hist. Ass.* (1902), I, 150; and see an illuminating discussion by Christopher C. Langdell in an article on *"The Status of Our New Territories"* in *Harvard Law Review* (1899), XII. The Constitution itself provided that it was to become effective *"between the States"* ratifying.

That it was the peoples of the separate States which adopted the Constitution was made clear when the first ten Amendments were adopted in 1789: the last of which stated that "the powers not delegated to the United States by the Constitution, nor prohibited by it to the States are reserved to the States respectively, or to the people." This power was not reserved to the States in a body, for there was no such body of States except as they united in the new Government, but to the States *respectively*.

The reservation of non-delegated power "to the people" as well as "to the States respectively" did not mean "to the people of the country collectively," but "to the people of each State." That this was so, is to be seen from the history of the manner in which these words "to the people" were inserted in the Amendment by Congress.

The Tenth Amendment, as introduced in the First Congress by James Madison, June 8, 1789, read as follows: "The powers not delegated by this Constitution nor prohibited by it to the States are reserved to the States respectively." This was a mere condensation of the Amendments which had been voted for by six State Conventions and by a meeting of minority members in one State as follows:

Massachusetts: "First. That it be explicitly declared, that all powers not expressly delegated by the aforesaid Constitution are reserved to the several States, to be by them exercised."

Maryland: "That Congress shall exercise no power but what is expressly delegated by this Constitution."

Virginia: "1st. That each State in the Union shall respectively retain every power, jurisdiction and right, which is not by this Constitution delegated to the Congress of the United States, or to the departments of the federal government."

"17th. That those clauses which declare that Congress shall not exercise certain powers, be not interpreted, in any manner whatsoever, to extend the powers of Congress; but that they may be construed either as making exceptions to the specified powers where this shall be the case, or otherwise, as inserted merely for greater caution."

South Carolina: "That no section or paragraph of the said Constitution warrants a construction that the States do not retain every power not expressly relinquished by them and vested in the General Government of the Union."

New Hampshire: "That it be explicitly declared that all powers not expressly and particularly delegated by the aforesaid Constitution are reserved to the several States, to be by them exercised."

New York: "That every power, jurisdiction and

right which is not by the said Constitution clearly delegated to the Congress of the United States or the departments of the Government thereof, remains to the People of the several States, or to their respective State Governments to whom they may have granted the same; and that those clauses in the said Constitution which declare that Congress shall have or exercise certain powers do not imply that Congress is entitled to any powers not given by the said Constitution; but such clauses are to be construed either as exceptions to certain specified powers, or as inserted merely for greater caution.

Pennsylvania (minority): "That Congress shall not exercise any powers whatever, but such as are expressly given to that body by the Constitution of the United States . . . but all the rights of sovereignty, which are not by the said Constitution expressly and plainly vested in the Congress, shall be deemed to remain with and shall be exercised by the several States in the Union, according to their respective Constitutions."

When Madison's Amendment was considered by Congress in the Committee of the Whole, on August 18, 1789, St. George Tucker of Virginia, a strong antifederalist, moved to amend by prefixing to it the following words: "all powers being derived from the people" and also by inserting before "delegated" the word "expressly." The motion was lost, owing to Madison's opposition to the use of the word "expressly." Thereupon Daniel Carroll of Maryland proposed that the words "or to the people" be added at the end of the Amendment; and this was agreed to without opposition.

It is evident that Carroll's amendment was intended merely as a renewal of the first part of Tucker's amendment and as a re-expression of the fact that the powers reserved were derived in each State from the people of the State.

When the Committee of the Whole reported to the House, no objection was raised to this change, and the Amendment was adopted, August 21, 1789, with no further change except that on the motion of Roger Sherman of Connecticut, the words "to the United States" were inserted after the word "delegated." *Annals of Congress*, 1st Cong., 1st Sess.

APPENDIX C

LIST OF INTER-STATE DECISIONS

1. *New York* v. *Conn.* (1799) 4 Dallas 1
   "   (1799) 4 Dallas 3
   "   (1799) 4 Dallas 6
2. *N. Jersey* v. *N. York* (1830) 3 Peters 461
   "   (1831) 5 Peters 284
   "   (1832) 6 Peters 323
3. *Rhode Island* v. *Mass.* (1833) 7 Peters 651
   "   (1837) 11 Peters 226
   "   (1838) 12 Peters 657
   "   (1838) 12 Peters 755
   "   (1839) 13 Peters 23
   "   (1840) 14 Peters 210
   "   (1841) 15 Peters 233
4. *Maryland* v. *Virginia* (1835) not reported,
                                     see 12 Peters 724
5. *Missouri* v. *Iowa* (1849) 7 Howard 660
   "   (1850) 10 Howard 1
   "   (1896) 160 U.S. 688
   "   (1897) 165 U.S. 118
6. *Florida* v. *Georgia* (1850) 11 Howard 293
   "   (1854) 17 Howard 478
7. *Alabama* v. *Georgia* (1860) 23 Howard 509
8. *Ky.* v. *Dennison, Gov.*
   of Ohio   (1861) 24 Howard 66
9. *Virginia* v. *W. Va.* (1871) 11 Wallace 39
10. *Missouri* v. *Ky.*   (1871) 11 Wallace 395
11. *S. Car.* v. *Georgia* (1876) 93 U.S. 4
12. *N. Hamp.* v. *La.*   (1883) 108 U.S. 76
13. *N. York* v. *La.*   (1883) 108 U.S. 76

14. *Indiana* v. *Kentucky* (1890) 136 U.S. 479
      "   (1895) 159 U.S. 275
      "   (1896) 163 U.S. 520
      "   (1897) 167 U.S. 270
15. *Nebraska* v. *Iowa*   (1892) 143 U.S. 359
      "   (1892) 145 U.S. 519
16. *Iowa* v. *Illinois*   (1893) 147 U.S. 1
      "   (1894) 151 U.S. 238
17. *Virginia* v. *Tenn.*   (1893) 148 U.S. 503
      "   (1895) 158 U.S. 267
      "   (1900) 177 U.S. 501
      "   (1903) 190 U.S. 64
18. *Louisiana* v. *Texas* (1900) 176 U.S. 1
19. *Missouri* v. *Illinois* (1901) 180 U.S. 208
      "   (1906) 200 U.S. 496
      "   (1906) 202 U.S. 598
20. *Kansas* v. *Colorado* (1902) 185 U.S. 125
      "   (1907) 206 U.S. 46
21. *S. Dak.* v. *N. Car.* (1904) 192 U.S. 286
22. *Missouri* v. *Nebraska* (1904) 196 U.S. 23
      "   (1905) 197 U.S. 577
23. *Louisiana* v. *Miss.* (1906) 202 U.S. 1
24. *Iowa* v. *Illinois*   (1906) 202 U.S. 59
25. *Virginia* v. *W. Va.* (1907) 206 U.S. 290
      "   (1908) 209 U.S. 514
      "   (1911) 220 U.S. 1
      "   (1911) 222 U.S. 17
      "   (1913) 231 U.S. 89
      "   (1914) 234 U.S. 117
      "   (1915) 238 U.S. 202
      "   (1916) 241 U.S. 531
      "   (1918) 246 U.S. 565
26. *Wash.* v. *Oregon*   (1908) 211 U.S. 127

APPENDIX C

"	(1909)	214 U.S. 205
27. *Missouri* v. *Kansas*	(1909)	213 U.S. 78
28. *Maryland* v. *W. Va.*	(1910)	217 U.S. 1
"	(1910)	217 U.S. 577
"	(1912)	225 U.S. 1
29. *N. Car.* v. *Tenn.*	(1914)	235 U.S. 1
"	(1916)	240 U.S. 652
30. *Arkansas* v. *Tenn.*	(1918)	246 U.S. 158
"	(1918)	247 U.S. 461
31. *Arkansas* v. *Miss.*	(1919)	250 U.S. 39
"	(1920)	252 U.S. 344
32. *Minnesota* v. *Wis.*	(1920)	252 U.S. 273
33. *N. York* v. *N. Jersey*	(1921)	256 U.S. 296
34. *Georgia* v. *S. Car.*	(1922)	257 U.S. 516
"	(1922)	259 U.S. 572
35. *Oklahoma* v. *Texas*	(1921)	256 U.S. 70
"	(1922)	258 U.S. 574
36 *Wyoming* v. *Colorado*	(1922)	259 U.S. 419
37. *Penn.* v. *W. Virginia*	(1923)	262 U.S. 553
38. *Ohio* v. *W. Virginia*	(1923)	262 U.S. 553
39. *N. Dak.* v. *Minnesota*	(1923)	263 U.S.

APPENDIX D

Proposed Legislation on Inter-state Suits

It was held, as early as 1796, in *Grayson* v. *Virginia*, 3 Dallas 320, that while the Court would not issue process to compel a State to enter an appearance, it would take jurisdiction of the case and proceed with it *ex parte*, if the State did not see fit to appear; see also *Huger* v. *South Carolina*, 3 Dallas 339, in 1797. For thirty years, however, representatives of the States contended that the Supreme Court had no power to take jurisdiction of suits against States, until Congress should have legislated and prescribed the method of procedure in such cases.

In the 13*th Cong.*, 2*nd Sess.*, Feb. 15, 1814, p. 632, Senator Bledsoe of Kentucky introduced a memorial of its Legislature praying "such provision as may be necessary for the purpose of regulating the jurisdiction and prescribing the mode of proceeding in controversy between the different States." In the House, a bill was reported "to prescribe the method of prosecuting and deciding controversies between two or more States." Gholson of Virginia, moved indefinite postponement which was favored by Humphreys, Grundy and Rhea of Tennessee, Wright of Maryland and Alston of Kentucky, and opposed by Hawkins, Montgomery, Desha and Sharp of Kentucky, Jackson of Virginia and Farrow of South Carolina, in a warm debate. The reporter states (pp. 2003-2004: "It appeared in the course of this debate that the necessity which had produced the memorial of Kentucky and, in consequence thereof, the intro-

duction of the bill before the House arose from the
existence of a controversy between the States of
Kentucky and Tennessee in relation to the boundary
line which dispute had commenced between the
mother States of Virginia and North Carolina . . .
and which, it appears, the two States could not accommodate; but, on the contrary, a settlement of
which becomes every day less practicable from the
lapse of time, irritation by repeated collision and the
value of the land which is in dispute having been
granted to different individuals at the same time by
both States. The discussion was not confined to the
abstract expediency of legislating on the subject of
the bill, but more or less connected itself with the
merit of the conflicting claims of Tennessee and
Kentucky to the land, the titles to which are jeopar-
dized and unsettled in consequence of this dispute.
An opinion was expressed by the members of Tennessee that the question may be amicably settled
without the intervention of such a law." Indefinite
postponement was voted, 86 to 27.

In the 15th Cong., 1st Sess., March 23, 1818, p.
278, a bill was reported in the Senate "prescribing
the mode of commencing, prosecuting and deciding
controversies between two or more States." On April
1, 1818, on motion of Campbell of Tennessee, it was
indefinitely postponed.

A similar bill was introduced in December, 1818,
and again indefinitely postponed, see 15th Cong.,
2nd Sess., pp. 74, 120.

The result of the failure of these bills was that
Kentucky and Tennessee settled their dispute by a

compact of February 2, 1820—see especially *Russell*
v. *American Association* (1917), 139 Tenn. 124.

In the 17*th Cong.*, 1*st Sess.*, Jan. 7, 1822, p. 53,
Senator Dickerson of New Jersey presented a resolution of the New Jersey Legislature praying for "the
passage of a law for the decision of territorial or
other controversies between States in such manner as
is authorized by the Constitution," since "Congress
have hitherto omitted to carry into effect the wise and
salutary provisions of the Constitution for that purpose by vesting adequate powers in the Courts of
the United States." A bill was reported in the Senate
providing that "in all cases where any matter of
controversy now exists or may hereafter exist between States in relation to jurisdiction, territory, or
boundaries, or any other matter which may be the
proper subject of judicial decision . . . the State
deeming itself aggrieved may file suit in the nature
of a bill in equity." On April 15, 1822 (p. 390),
Senator Southard of New Jersey argued at length the
long standing controversy between New Jersey and
New York. Senator Van Buren denied the necessity
of any legislation, as the contested questions could be
brought up in a suit between individuals of the two
States. On April 17 (p. 394), Senators King and
Van Buren of New York, Barbour of Virginia, and
Macon of North Carolina argued, without going into
the merits, "that such a bill ought not to pass without
some apparent necessity, and as its passage did not
appear indispensable, it would be impolitic, as consequences might grow out of it of much political in-
convenience." Senator Dickerson of New Jersey of-

fered to confine the operation of the bill to pending disputes between New Jersey and New York and New Jersey and Delaware; but the bill failed of passage.

Similar bills were introduced in Congress in 1828 by New Jersey, and by Rhode Island in 1830; but no action was ever taken on them.

APPENDIX E

ACTS OF CONGRESS GIVING CONSENT TO COMPACTS BETWEEN STATES

Act of Feb. 4, 1791 (1 Stat. 189) admitting Kentucky into the Union. Virginia-Kentucky compact of Dec. 18, 1789.

Resolution of May 12, 1820 (3 Stat. 609). Kentucky and Tennessee, February 2, 1820. Boundary Line.

Act of June 28, 1834 (4 Stat. 708). New York and New Jersey, September 16, 1833. Boundary Line, execution of process, etc.

Act of January 3, 1855 (10 Stat. 602). Massachusetts and New York, May 14, and July 21, 1853. Cession of District of Boston Corner by Massachusetts to New York.

Act of February 9, 1858 (11 Stat. 382). Massachusetts and Rhode Island. Attorney General directed to assent to agreement between States in adjustment of boundary dispute before Supreme Court.

Joint Resolution of Feb. 21, 1861 (12 Stat. 250). Arkansas, Louisiana and Texas. Joint action for removal of raft from Red River (past or prospective agreements).

Joint Resolution of March 10, 1866 (14 Stat. 350). Virginia and West Virginia. Cession of Berkeley and Jefferson Counties to West Virginia.

Act of March 3, 1879 (20 Stat. 481). Virginia and Maryland, Jan. 16, 1877. Boundary Line.

Act of April 7, 1880 (21 Stat. 72). New York and

Vermont, Nov. 27, 1876, and March 20, 1879. Boundary Line.

Act of Feb. 26, 1881 (21 Stat. 351). New York and Connecticut, Dec. 8, 1879. Boundary Line.

Act of Oct. 12, 1888 (25 Stat. 553). Connecticut and Rhode Island, May 25, 1887. Boundary Line.

Act of Aug. 19, 1890 (26 Stat. 329). New York and Pennsylvania, March 26, 1896. Boundary Line.

Act of July 24, 1897 (30 Stat. 214). South Dakota and Nebraska, June 3, and June 7, 1897. Boundary Line.

Joint Resolution of March 3, 1901 (31 Stat. 1465). Tennessee and Virginia. Jan. 28, and Feb. 9, 1901. Boundary Line.

Act of March 1, 1905 (33 Stat. 820). South Dakota and Nebraska. Boundary Line.

Act of Jan. 24, 1907 (34 Stat. 858). New Jersey and Delaware, March 21, 1905. Jurisdiction over Delaware River, process, etc.

Joint Resolution of Jan. 26, 1909 (35 Stat. 1160). Mississippi and Louisiana. Boundary Line and criminal jurisdiction (prospective agreement).

Joint Resolution of Jan. 26, 1909 (35 Stat. 1161). Mississippi and Arkansas. Boundary Line and criminal jurisdiction (prospective agreement).

Joint Resolution of Feb. 4, 1909 (35 Stat. 1163). Tennessee and Arkansas. Boundary Line and criminal jurisdiction (prospective agreement).

Joint Resolution of June 10, 1910 (36 Stat. 881). Missouri and Kansas. Boundary Line and criminal jurisdiction (prospective agreement).

Joint Resolution of June 10, 1910 (36 Stat. 881).

Oregon and Washington. Boundary Line (prospective agreement).

Joint Resolution of June 22, 1910 (36 Stat. 882). Wisconsin, Illinois, Indiana and Michigan. Criminal jurisdiction on Lake Michigan (prospective agreement).

Act of March 1, 1911 (36 Stat. 961). General consent to agreements between States for conservation of forests.

Act of Oct. 3, 1914 (38 Stat. 727). Massachusetts and Connecticut, March 19, 1908, and June 6, 1913. Boundary Line.

Act of Aug. 8, 1917 (40 Stat. 266 Sec. 5). Minnesota and North and South Dakota authorized to make agreements for improvement of navigation and control of floods on boundary waters and tributaries.

Act of April 8, 1918 (40 Stat. 515). Oregon and Washington, protection of fish in Columbia River, etc. (Oregon, Laws 1915, Chap. 188, Sec. 20.)

Act of September 13, 1918 (40 Stat. 959). Wisconsin and Minnesota, April 9, 1917, and March 26, 1917. Mutual cessions of territory.

Act of July 11, 1919 (41 Stat. 158). New York and New Jersey, construction of tunnel under Hudson River (prospective, authorized by New Jersey, Laws 1918, Chap. 49, 50, and New York, Session Laws 1919, Chap. 70, and General Laws 1919, Chap. 178).

Act of Aug. 19, 1921 (42 Stat. 171). Arizona, California, Colorado, Nevada, New Mexico, Utah and Wyoming authorized to negotiate and enter into

agreement for equitable apportionment of waters
of Colorado River and its tributaries. Such agreement to be made by Jan. 1, 1923, and to be subject to approval by the legislature of each State
concerned and by Congress.

Joint Resolution, Aug. 23, 1921 (42 Stat. 174-180).
New York and New Jersey creation of "Port of
New York Authority" for comprehensive development of port of New York. Supplement to agreement of 1834, noted above.

Joint Resolution of July 1, 1922 (42 Stat. 822-826).
New York and New Jersey, supplemental agreement embodying comprehensive plan for development of port of New York.

Joint Resolution of Sept. 22, 1922 (42 Stat. 1058).
Kansas and Missouri, development of waterworks
plants at Kansas City, Kansas, and Kansas City,
Missouri.

NOTES

[1] Ellsworth termed this government "a Federal Society united by a charter." *Elliot's Debates*, V, July 23, 1787. Note *ibid.*, June 5, 1787, speeches of Gerry and King declaring that these Articles were ratified in some of the Eastern States by the people of the States, while the Southern States ratified through their respective Legislatures; and as to the submission of the Articles to the people of Massachusetts by the Legislature of the State, see especially *The People's Law or Popular Participation in Law Making* (1909) by Charles S. Lobingier, 167, 168, 180.

[2] *Warren-Adams Letters, Mass. Hist. Soc. Coll.* (1917), Adams to James Warren, Aug. 17, 1776; *Massachusetts Centinel*, April 2, 1785.

[3] The Declaration of Independence had declared "that these United Colonies are, and of right ought to be, free and independent States . . . and as free and independent States, they have full power to levy war, and to do all other acts and things which independent States may of right do"; and the sovereignty of the King, as James Monroe said, had "passed directly to the people of each Colony, and not to the people of all the Colonies in the aggregate; to thirteen distinct communities, and not to one." *The Writings of James Monroe* (1902), VI, 224.

In *Nathan* v. *Commonwealth of Virginia* (1781), 1 Dallas 77, the State Court of Pennsylvania held Virginia to be a sovereign, independent State. In *Ware* v. *Hylton* (1796) 3 Dallas 199, 224. Chase, J., said: "A declaration, not that the United Colonies jointly in a collective capacity were independent States, etc., but that each of them was a sovereign and independent State." In *McIlvaine* v. *Coxe* (1808), 4 Cranch 209, 212, Cushing, J., said: "The several States which composed this Union, became entitled, from the time they declared themselves independent, to all the rights and powers of sovereign States." In *Rhode Island* v. *Massachusetts* (1838), 12 Peters, p. 751; Baldwin, J., said: "The Revolution devolved on each State the prerogative of the King as he had held it in the Colonies."

NOTES

In the Federal Convention of June 19, 1787, Wilson and Hamilton had taken a different view and held that the States became independent, *not individually but unitedly;* Charles C. Pinckney also said in the South Carolina Legislature in 1788: "This admirable manifesto sufficiently refutes the doctrine of the individual sovereignty and independence of the several States. The separate independence and individual sovereignty of the several States were never thought of by the enlightened band of patriots who framed this Declaration . . . a species of political heresy." See also *The Jubilee of the Constitution* (1839) by John Quincy Adams. Such, however, was not the general view held in the respective States. As Chief Justice Taney said in *Kentucky* v. *Dennison* (1861), 24 Howard 66: "The Confederation was only a league of separate sovereignties, in which each State, within its own limits, held and exercised all the powers of sovereignty."

[4] *Life of Elbridge Gerry* (1828), by James T. Austin, II, 167, Jay to Gerry, Jan. 9, 1782. Jay wrote to Livingston from Paris, Dec. 14, 1782: "The boundaries between the States should be immediately settled and all causes of discord between them removed." *The Correspondence and Public Papers of John Jay*, III, 6.

[5] *Writings of Benjamin Franklin* (1904), VI, 420, draft of a Confederation of July 21, 1775. A Committee of Congress reported on Aug. 30, 1776, an Article, based on the first draft of the Articles of Confederation made by John Dickinson of Delaware on the preceding July 12, as follows: "The United States assembled shall have the sole and exclusive right and power of . . . settling all disputes and differences now subsisting or that may hereafter arise between two or more Colonies concerning boundaries, jurisdiction or any other cause whatever." It was not until Oct. 27, 1777, that a final agreement was reached as to the method of treating these State controversies.

Samuel Adams wrote to Gen. James Warren, Oct. 29, 1777: "Most of the important Articles are agreed to. Each State claims the sovereignty and independence. Every power, jurisdiction and right which is not by the Confederation, expressly delegated to the United States in Congress assembled. . . . All disputes about boundaries are to be decided by Judges to be appointed in the following mode." *Letters of Members of the Continental Congress*, II, 536.

Thomas Burke, a delegate to Congress from North Carolina wrote, Nov. 18, 1777, that this Article IX, providing for appeal to Congress and a Court was badly drawn: "I have no idea of an appeal or last resort unless there be some prior jurisdiction and prior resort, and I know of no such thing between the States. . . . If the Congress are to nominate the persons who constitute the Judiciary, I can easily foresee it will not always, if ever, be impartial. . . . That State which has the prevailing interest in Congress will thus nominate all the Judges. . . . If this Article were amended by giving the nomination by ballot to the States not interested, it would answer better to my idea of an impartial arbiter between the States . . . as it now stands they (the Congress) have it too much in their power to influence the decisions which they themselves are to execute, which in my opinion is dangerous in any political community." *Ibid*, II, 555.

Henry Laurens of South Carolina, President of the Congress, wrote to John Rutledge, President of South Carolina, Dec. 1, 1777: "I beg leave to remark to my late Colleagues that Congress before printing judged it proper to make several essential alterations particularly in Article 9th, parag. 2d.,—that I have therefore no cause to blush at the appearance of my name among the few Nays in the original vote. I should be still better pleased to see that Article undergo a little further amendment." *Ibid*, II, 578.
[6] That the people of those days had not become used to regarding this tribunal as a Court is shown in newspaper accounts of other suits brought before it. Thus the *American Herald* (Boston), Feb. 7, 1785, published a despatch from Hartford, Conn. "We are informed that the controversy between the States of Massachusetts and New York respecting the western territory of unlocated lands is submitted by order of Congress to *arbitration*. Who the *auditors are*, we have not heard, except that John Rutledge, Esq., the Governor of South Carolina is one."

The suit of *Pennsylvania* v. *Connecticut* was thus referred to in *Massachusetts Centinel*, Oct. 27, 1784: "Agree-

NOTES

able to the Articles of Confederation, Commissioners for settling the right of territory of the respective claimants sat some time since, who adjudged it to be long of right to Pennsylvania." The suit was referred in the Proclamation of the President and Supreme Executive Council of Pennsylvania, Jan. 1, 1783, as follows: "Whereas the Court of Commissioners constituted and declared by the United States in Congress assembled." *Pennsylvania Journal*, Jan. 11, 1783.

[7] See especially *Critical Period of American History* (1908), by John Fiske, 152, 156, for map and authorities cited; see also *Letters of Members of the Continental Congress* I, 229; II, 320.

[8] David Brearly and William Churchill Houston of New Jersey, William Whipple of New Hampshire, Welcome Arnold of Rhode Island, and Cyrus Griffin of Virginia were the Judges in 1782, in *Pennsylvania v. Connecticut*, of whom William Whipple was chosen "President" of the Court. James Wilson, William Bradford, Joseph Reed and Jonathan D. Sargent, represented the plaintiff State and William Samuel Johnson, Eliphalet Dyer and Jesse Root, the defendant.

[9] *The Judicial Settlement of Controversies between States of the American Union: An Analysis of Cases decided in the Supreme Court of the United States* (1919), by James Brown Scott; *The United States of America: A Study in International Organization* (1920), by James Brown Scott, p. 324, letter of Livingston to Lafayette, Jan. 10, 1783. No writer on the subject of these lectures can fail to acknowledge his great indebtedness to Dr. Scott for the above books.

See also Resolution of the Council of Censors of Sept. 14, 1784, in *Massachusetts Centinel*, Nov. 6, 1784; editorial in *Freeman's Journal* (Philadelphia), Jan. 21, 1783.

[10] Washington to Lafayette, Feb. 7, 1788, *Records of the Federal Convention*, by Max Farrand, III; *ibid.* to Mrs. Macaulay Graham, Nov. 16, 1787: "The various and opposite interests which were to be conciliated, the local prejudices which were to be subdued, the diversity of opinions and sentiments which were to be reconciled, and, in fine, the sacrifices which were necessary to be made on all sides

[128]

for the general welfare, combined to make it a work of so
intricate and difficult a nature, that I think it is much to
be wondered at, that anything could have been produced
with such unanimity as the Constitution proposed."

A New York correspondent wrote to the *Independent
Chronicle*, in Boston, July 19, 1787: "What feuds, what
discords do we behold from the several quarters of the
United States. While those in the East only *appear* to be
dying away, new and accumulated evils seem to be gather-
ing in the West."

Charles Turner said in the Massachusetts Convention,
in February, 1788: "Considering the great diversity of
local interests, views and habits—Considering the un-
paralleled variety of sentiments among the citizens of the
United States—I despair of obtaining a more perfect Constitution than this, at present."

[11] See *American State Papers Misc.*, I, 81, 114, in the
House, April 1, Dec. 23, 1794; the proposal was apparently
defeated as it does not appear in the final Act of Con-
gress of March 3, 1795, c. 50 (1 Stat. 443), In the 31st
Cong., 1st Sess., however, on motion made in the House,
Dec. 24, 1859, to print 15,000 copies of President Taylor's
message, a motion to print 5,000 extra copies in the Ger-
man language was unanimously carried. See also *The
German Element in the United States* (1909), by Albert
Bernhardt Faust; *The Scotch-Irish* (1902), by Charles A.
Hanna, I, 81-83; *Autobiography of Thomas Jefferson
Coolidge, Mass. Hist. Soc. Pub.* (1923), p. 28.

[12] See *American Herald* (Boston) March 29, 1784, proclamation of March 26, 1784, which, so far as known, has not
been republished before. It is to be noted that Thomas
Chittenden, Governor of Vermont, wrote to the President
of Congress, April 26, 1784, with reference to a resolution
of the New York Legislature: "As to this bloody proposition the Council of this State have only to remark that
Vermont does not wish to enter into a war with the State
of New York, but that she will act on the defensive and
expects that Congress and the twelve States will observe
a strict neutrality and let the contending States settle
their own controversy." *Massachusetts Centinel*, Dec. 4,
1784. See also as to the Vermont war, *Independent Chron-*

icle (Boston), Feb. 26, March 25, April 27, 1784; and see *Making the Republic of Vermont,* in *Amer. Antiq. Soc. Proc.* XXXI.

[13] See *Royal Gazette* (N.Y.), Jan. 11, 1783: "The six colonies of Georgia, North Carolina, South Carolina, Virginia, Delaware and New Hampshire have very sagaciously withheld all contribution; whilst, as it appears, Pennsylvania *alone* has paid in above a third part of the whole sum that is to come in, and nearly as much as all the four Colonies of New England together, who were so greatly benefited by their captures and commerce in the early stages of the war. A war begun to please Boston Polticians! who now shrink from the general burden, by the artifice of their late laws, to discount debts of the Colony to their own people, against the taxes demanded by Congress for the common use of the Continent. They will, however, neither escape the vigilance nor vengeance of the other branches of the Confederacy, if the Independency can be maintained. And it is left to conjecture how far the spirit of resentment for the defalcations of Connecticut has already influenced to the recent decision in Congress against the claims of that Colony, to all lands beyond New Jersey through the heart of the Continent to the Pacific Ocean. A claim set up by the Susquehanna Company, a party of land-jobbers, whose distrust of success under the government of Great Britain led them to wish for that separation, which has already dashed down their flattering expectations of becoming the most powerful and populous as well as extensive party in the league."

[14] John Jay wrote from Paris, to Elbridge Gerry, Feb. 19, 1784: "A report prevails that Connecticut will not acquiesce in the late decision of her controversy with Pennsylvania. They who fear our being a united and consequently a formidable people (and I can hardly tell who do not fear it) rejoice at this intelligence." Francis Dana wrote from Annapolis to Gerry, April 28, 1784: "The first we shall take up will probably be the appointment of a federal Court upon the claims of the citizens of Connecticut and of Pennsylvania. Mr. (James) Wilson has already arrived upon that business." *Life of Elbridge Gerry* (1828), by James T. Austin, II. See also *Independ-*

ent Chronicle, April 1, 1784: "We hear that Congress have granted the Susquehanna Company a trial for the right of soil to our western lands."

The practical operation of the Court under the Articles of Confederation was well expressed by James Wilson in the Pennsylvania Convention in 1787, arguing for a Court with power to enforce: "I have, with pleasing emotion, seen the wisdom and beneficence of a less efficient power . . . in the determination of the controversy between Pennsylvania and Connecticut; but I have lamented that the authority of Congress did not extend to extinguish entirely the spark which has kindled a dangerous flame in the district of Wyoming. . . . After much altercation, expense of time and considerable expense of money, the State was successful enough to obtain a decree in its favor . . . but what was the consequence? The Congress had no power to carry the decree into execution. Hence the distraction and animosity which have ever since prevailed."

[15] Pennsylvania disputed with Maryland her Southern line; and with Virginia, title to Western lands, so that if Virginia had prevailed, Pittsburgh would now be a Virginian city; but the dispute was temporarily settled by agreement in 1784; and for a case involving a tract of land in the territory disputed between Pennsylvania and Virginia, in Allegheny County, see *Marlatt* v. *Silk* (1837), 11 Peters 1. The controversy was settled by a compact between the two States in 1870, see *Early Virginia Claims in Pennsylvania*, by G. T. J. Chapman, *Mag. of Amer. Hist.* (1882), VIII.

New York contested with Pennsylvania the outlet to Lake Erie. New Jersey contested with Pennsylvania rights to islands in and land under the Delaware River. A dispute between New Hampshire and New York, giving rise to armed conflict was only settled by the admission of Vermont as a State in 1791; see especially Hildreth's *History of the United States*, III, 407 et seq, *The New Hampshire Grants*, by John L. Rice, *Mag. of Amer. Hist.* (1882), VIII. New York and Massachusetts contested the ownership of 3,000,000 acres in Western New York and settled it by compact in 1786. New York and Connecticut had a similar contest. A controversy between Delaware and New Jersey over islands in the Delaware River, was not settled until 1849, when it was submitted to arbitration by John Sergeant of Philadelphia, who decided in favor of Delaware's contention in the famous *Pea Patch Case*, see 1 Wallace, Jr. Virginia and North Carolina were at odds as to their mountain boundary; Virginia and Maryland had a bitter conflict over the navigation and jurisdiction over the Potomac River; see the compact between Virginia and Maryland in 1785, with reference to trade and navigation on the Potomac River, and see especially *Wharton* v. *Wise* (1894), 153 U.S. 155; see also *Georgetown* v. *Alexandria Canal Co.* (1838), 12 Peters 91; *Marine Railway Co.* v. *United States* (1921), 257 U.S. 47; *Maryland* v. *West Virginia* (1910), 217 U.S. 1; see also assent of Congress to award of arbitrators based on the compact of 1785, Act of March 3, 1879 (20 Stat. 481). Virginia and New Jersey had also a bitter conflict over lands West of Pennsylvania known as Indiana.

A letter from Carter Braxton of Virginia to Landon Carter from Philadeplhia, April 14, 1776, describes the conditions between the States then existing, as follows: "The Colonies of Massachusetts and Connecticut . . . have claims on the Province of Pennsylvania in the whole for near one-third of the land within their Provincial bounds, and indeed the claim extended to its full extent comes within four miles of this city. This dispute was carried to the King and Council, and with them it now lies. The Eastern Colonies, unwilling they should now be the Arbiter, have asserted their claims by force and have at this time eight hundred men in arms upon the upper part of this land called Wyoming, where they are peaceable at present only through the influence of Congress. Then naturally there arises a heart-burning and jealousy between these people, and they must have, too, very different objects in view. The Province of New York is not without her fears and apprehensions, from the temper of her neighbors, . . . Even Virginia is not free from claim in Pennsylvania, nor Maryland from those in Virginia. Some of the Delegates of our Colony carry their ideas of right to lands so far to the eastward that the middle Col-

NOTES

onies dread their being swallowed up between the claims
of them and those from the East. . . . I am convinced the
assertion of Independence is far off. If it was to be now
asserted, the Continent would be torn in pieces by intestine
wars and convulsions. Previous to Independence, all disputes must be healed and harmony prevail. A grand Continental League must be formed and a superintending
power." *Letters of Members of the Continental Congress,*
I.

¹⁶ See McHenry's note on Randolph's speech, May 29,
1787, *Farrand,* I, 26; *Elliot's Debates,* V, Aug. 29, 1787;
ibid., II, 236; *ibid.,* III, 30, 75-6, 82, 571.

See also *Boston Gazette,* Dec. 2, 1782, letter from Hartford, Conn., to Springfield, Mass., Nov. 23: "I have
nothing new to communicate except that our State seems
determined to resent the injustice of yours in establishing
so iniquitous a law as the Pine Board Act. Judgment cannot be obtained within our Courts for the recovery of any
debts due to persons within your State, and the reasons assigned for withholding it is that no debt can be recovered
from you but in the worst articles specified in the aforesaid Act." In 1786, however, a bill was defeated in the
Connecticut Legislature, "excluding the inhabitants of the
State of Massachusetts Bay from a right to bring any
civil suit in their State, during the present prostration of
law and justice in that State." See *Massachusetts Centinel,*
Oct. 25, 1786.

In March, 1787, the Rhode Island Legislature passed an
Act excluding citizens of Connecticut from the benefit of
laws of Rhode Island relative to the tender of paper
money; thereupon Connecticut passed a law excluding
citizens of Rhode Island from the right to sue in the
Courts of Connecticut, see letter from Hartford, in *Virginia Independent Chronicle,* March 18, 1789.

¹⁷ "Our new Congress met a few days since at New York.
As this Great Head of the Confederation, we are taught
to look up to them for the administration of relief to our
languid and declining commerce. But alas! their hands are
tied—they are not permitted to do well, for fear they
should do ill. Our conduct to that august body is strangely
inconsistent; we, in effect, tell them they shall be rulers,

NOTES

but they shall not rule." *Massachusetts Centinel*, Dec. 3, 1785.

Elbridge Gerry wrote to James Monroe, June 11, 1787: "Unless a system of government is adopted by compact, force, I expect, will plant the standard, for such an anarchy as now exists cannot last long." *Documentary History of the Constitution*, IV, 199. Nathan Dane wrote to Rufus King, July 5, 1787: "You know the general opinion is that our Federal Constitution, must be mended; and if the Convention do not agree at least in some amendments, a universal despair of our keeping together will take place." *The Life and Correspondence of Rufus King* (1894).

[18] *Reflections on the Revolution in France* (1790), *Burke's Works*, V, 72.

[19] William Samuel Johnson noted the daily weather in his diary, and set down twenty-nine hot or very hot days out of the seventy-nine week days when he was in Philadelphia, and thirteen rainy days. See *Farrand*, III, 552.

[20] The Princeton graduates were: Alexander S. Martin of the Class of 1756; William Paterson, '63; Oliver Ellsworth, '66; Luther Martin, '66; William C. Houston, '68; Gunning Bedford, '71; James Madison, '71; Jonathan Dayton, '76; William R. Davie, '76; David Brearly also held an honorary degree from Princeton in 1781.

[21] *Pennsylvania Journal* (Philadelphia), Aug. 25, 1787; *Pennsylvania Herald*, May 30, 1787; *Independent Chronicle*, June 14, 1787; *Connecticut Courant*, June 11, 1787; *Virginia Independent Chronicle*, June 13, 1787; *New Hampshire Spy*, June 9, 12, 1787; *Independent Gazetteer* (Philadelphia), Aug. 6, 1787.

[22] *History of the Rise, Progress and Termination of the American Revolution* (1805), by Mercy Warren, III, 367 note; letter of "Rusticus," in *New York Journal*, Sept. 13, 1787.

See also letter of "Helvidius Priscus" in *Independent Chronicle* (Boston), Dec. 27, 1788, the pseudonym probably being that of Gen. James Warren (as asserted in the *Massachusetts Gazette*, March 14, 1788), though Christopher Gore wrote to Rufus King, Dec. 30, 1787, that it might be Samuel Adams. "It is well known that some of

the late Convention were the professed advocates of the
British system, that others stood suspended *in equilibrio*,
uncertain on which side to declare until the scale of fortune balanced in favour of America; that the political
maneuvers of some of them have always sunk in the vortex of private interest; and that the immense wealth of
others has set them above all principle. . . . How many
of the disinterested worthies who ventured everything
for the support of the rights of their country and the
liberties of mankind will be left to adorn that Assembly,
who have, ambitiously and daring, presumed (without any
commission for that purpose) to annihilate the sovereignties of the thirteen United States, to establish a Draconian
Code, and to bind posterity by their secret councils? It
may perhaps be replied that one-third part of the body
were of this generous description. . . . Several of them
left the Assembly, in disgust, before the decision of the
question: others expressly reprobated the proceedings of
a conclave where it has been ridiculously asserted all the
wisdom of America was concentered. And a Randolph,
Mason and Gerry had the firmness to avow their dissent."

That the Virginia delegates were not popular in Massachusetts may be seen from the comments as to characteristics of delegates to the previous Convention at Annapolis. Thus, Elbridge Gerry wrote to Rufus King, May 9,
1785 (King, I, 96): "What is the matter with Virginia?
Their attachments to their opinions originate, I fear, from
mistaken ideas of their own importance. They have certainly many good qualities; but has not their ambition
been bribed by artifice and flattery to besiege and under-
mine their reason and good policy?" And Stephen Hig-
ginson wrote to John Adams in July, 1786 (*Amer. Hist.
Ass.*, 1896, I, 733), as to the Annapolis Convention: "There
will be from New York Mr. Duane, Mr. Hamilton, Mr.
Chancellor Livingston. From Pennsylvania, Mr. Robert
Morris, Mr. Fitzsimmons, Mr. George Clymer. From
Virginia, Mr. Randolph, Mr. Madison, Judge Jones and
several others from those States, of like political principles
and characters. The measure appears to have originated in
Virginia and with Mr. Madison. The men I have mentioned are all of them esteemed great aristocrats and their

constituents know that such is their character. Very few of them have been in the commercial line, nor is it probable they know or care much about commercial objects."

Connecticut was also in disfavor with Massachusetts; and Gerry wrote to King, May 27, 1785: "The Devil is in that State. They are like a young puritan (since the establishment of our Independence) who, having been trammeled with piety from his birth and been just freed from his domestic confinement, runs into every excess, religious, moral and political."

23 *Works of Benjamin Franklin* (1904), XI, Franklin to Thomas Jordan, May 18, 1787: "I received your very kind letter of February 27th, together with the cask of porter you have been so good as to send me. We have at present what the French call *une assemblée des notables*, a convention composed of some of the principal people from the several States of our Confederation. They did me the honor of dining with me last Wednesday, when the cask was broached, and its contents met with the most cordial reception and universal approbation. In short, the company agreed unanimously that it was the best porter they had ever tasted."

A Massachusetts visitor to Philadelphia recorded in his diary that after a visit to Dr. Franklin's, "we took our leave at ten and I returned to my lodgings (at the Indian Queen). The gentlemen who lodged in the House were just sitting down to supper, a sumptuous table was spread, and the attendance in the style of noblemen. Mr. (Caleb) Strong came in and invited me to their hall where we sat till twelve." *Life, Journals and Correspondence of Manasseh Cutler* (1888), I. See also *The Framers of the Constitution*, by Martha J. Lamb, *Mag. of Amer. Hist.* (1885), XIII, 315-45.

24 *Independent Gazetteer* (Philadelphia), May 21, 23, 29, 1787.

25 North Carolina Delegates to Gov. Caswell, June 14, 1787, *Farrand*, III, 46; *History of the Foundation of the Constitution* (1882), by George Bancroft, II, 424, Mason to George Mason, Jr., June 1, 1787. *Independent Chronicle* (Boston), June 28, 1787.

26 It has been said that the room downstairs is where the

Convention sat. But see *Farrand*, III, 552, quoting *Life, Journals and Correspondence of Manasseh Cutler*, I: "From Mr. Peale's we went to the State House. This is a noble building; the architecture is in a richer and grander style than any public building I have ever before seen. The first story is not an open walk as is usual in buildings of this kind. In the middle, however, is a very broad cross aisle, and the floor above supported by two rows of pillars. From this aisle is a broad opening to a large hall, toward the west end, which opening is supported by arches and pillars. In this hall, the Courts are held and as you pass the aisle, you have a full view of the Court. The Supreme Court are now sitting. This bench consists of only three judges. Their robes are scarlet; the lawyers' black. The Chief Judge, Mr. McKean, was sitting with his hat on, which is the custom, but struck me as being very odd, and seemed to derogate from the dignity of a judge. The hall east of the aisle is employed for public business. The chamber over it is now occupied by the Continental Convention which is now sitting, but sentries are planted near —who appear to be very alert in the performance of their duty. Dr. Franklin lives in Market Street, between Second and Third Streets." See also *Farrand*, III, 553 note quoting *Annals of Philadelphia and Pennsylvania* (1855), by John T. Watson, I, 402: "The Convention met *upstairs*, and at the same time, the Chestnut Street pavement was covered with earth to silence the rattling of wheels."

See also *Pennsylvania Journal*, Aug. 25, 1787; *Boston Gazette*, Sept. 3, 1787; *Salem Mercury*, Sept. 4, 1787: "The punctuality with which the members of the Convention assemble every day at a certain hour, and the long time they spend in the deliberations of each day (sometimes seven hours) are proofs, among other things, how much they are entitled to the universal confidence of the people of America."

[27] *Boston Gazette*, May 23, 28, 1787; *Pennsylvania Packet*, May 18, 1787; *Maryland Journal*, May 22, 1787; *Salem Mercury*, May 29, 1787; *Freeman's Oracle* (Portsmouth, N.H.), May 26, 1787.

Expectations as to the action of the Convention ran high, long before it met. Thus the *Massachusetts Gazette*,

Jan. 12, 1787, published a Philadelphia despatch of Dec. 30, 1786: "A correspondent observes that every true patriot must be pleased with the very respectable delegation appointed by Virginia to meet in convention for federal purposes in this city on May next—Washington, Wythe and Randolph will be forever held in the highest veneration by every lover of American liberty. . . . A convention composed of such and similar characters will undoubtedly be able to remove the defects of the Confederation, produce a vigorous and energetic continental government which will crush and destroy faction, subdue insurrections, revive publick and private credit, disappoint our transatlantick enemies and their lurking emissaries among us, and finally (to use an Indian phrase) endure 'while the sun shines and the rivers flow.' "

Just before the opening of the Convention, a Philadelphia correspondent in the *Massachusetts Gazette*, of May 22, 1787, wrote: "As the time approaches for opening the business of the Federal Convention, it is natural that every lover of his country should experience some anxiety for the fate of an expedient so necessary and so precarious. Upon the event of this great council, indeed, depends everything that can be essential to the dignity and stability of the national character. The veteran who has toiled in the field, the statesman who has labored in the Cabinet, and every man who participates in the blessings of American Independence must feel that all the glory of the past and all the fortune of the future are involved in the momentous undertaking."

[28] "Such circumspection and secrecy mark the proceedings . . . that the members find it difficult to acquire the habits of communication even among themselves, and are so cautious in defeating the curiosity of the publick, that all debate is suspended on the entrance of their own inferior officers. . . . The anxiety of the people must be necessarily increased by every appearance of mystery in conducting this important business." *Boston Gazette*, June 11, 1787; *Virginia Independent Chronicle*, June 20, 1787.

Madison wrote to Jefferson, July 18: "The public mind is very impatient for the event, and various reports are circulating which tend to inflame curiosity. I do not learn, however, that any discontent is expressed at the concealment." *Doc. Hist.*, IV, 266.

"Extracts of letters, pieces and paragraphs innumerable have filled the papers upon the result of their national consultations; but as the most absolute secrecy has been maintained by that august assembly these paragraphs, etc., must be viewed as idle, the chimeras of the several political fancies which brought them forth." *New Hampshire Spy*, Sept. 1, 1787. Jeremy Belknap wrote to Ebenezer Hazard, Sept. 4, 1787: "Such has been their secrecy that I believe not an article of the Constitution is known, but if it should prove only a tolerable one, I think every friend to the peace and happiness of America should give it his support." *Belknap Papers, Mass. Hist. Soc. Coll.*

"The result of the Federal Convention has at length transpired, after a profound secrecy being observed by the members who composed it, which, at least, has done honor to their fidelity, as we believe that scarcely another example can be advanced of the same caution among so large a number of persons." *Pennsylvania Journal*, Oct. 6, 1787.

That the secrecy of the convention was not everywhere approved is seen from a letter by "Centinel" in the *Independent Gazetteer*, October, 1787: "The injunction of secrecy imposed on the members of the late Convention during their deliberation was obviously dictated by the genius of Aristocracy: it was deemed impolitic to unfold the principles of the intended government to the people, as this would have frustrated the end in view."

[29] A fictitious, detailed account of the "matters under consideration" in the Convention appeared in the *New York Daily Advertiser*, Aug. 13, 1787, in a letter from a "gentleman in Philadelphia to his friend in Charleston, So. Car., dated July 4, 1787."

Another ridiculous report was circulated from New Haven, Conn. It appeared in the *Pennsylvania Packet*, Aug. 13, *Independent Gazetteer*, Aug. 14, *Independent Chronicle*, Aug. 16, *Maryland Journal*, Aug. 17, 1787, and in many other papers as follows: "A circular letter is handing about the country recommending a kingly government for these States. The writer proposes to send to

England for the Bishop of Osnaburgh, second son of the King of Great Britain, and have him crowned King over this continent. We have found, by experience, says he, that we have not wit enough to govern ourselves, that all our declamation and parade about Republicanism, Liberty, Property and the Rights of Man are mere stuff and non-sense, and that it is high time for us to tread back the way-ward path we have walked in these twelve years. This plan, we are told, gains friends and partisans rapidly, and it surely is necessary for the great body of the people to be on their guard. The Federal Convention may save us from this worst of all curses (a Royal Government) if we are wise enough to adopt their recommendation when they shall be communicated to us." The authorship of this report was investigated by Alexander Hamilton; see letters of Hamilton to Jeremiah Wadsworth, Aug. 20, Wadsworth to Hamilton, Aug. 26, D. Humphreys to Hamilton, Sept. 1, 16, saying that the article was first printed in a Fairfield, Conn., paper July 25, 1787. *Doc. Hist.,* IV, 255, 265, 267; see also *Constitutional History of the United States,* by George Ticknor Curtis, I, 624, note. It was regarded so seriously that a semi-official denial was made by the Convention as follows: "We are well informed that many letters have been written to the members of the Convention, from different quarters, respecting the reports idly circulating, that it is intended to establish a monarchical government, to send for the Bishop of Osnaburgh, etc., etc.,—to which it has been uniformly answered: 'Though we cannot, affirmatively, tell you what we are doing, we can negatively, tell you what we are not doing—we never once thought of a King.'" *Boston Gazette,* Aug. 27, 1787.

Substantially the only correct item as to the Convention's actions was published in the *Pennsylvania Packet,* July 31, 1787 (and copied in many papers): "The Federal Convention having resolved upon the measures necessary to discharge their important trust adjourned until Monday next (i.e., from July 26 to Aug. 6) in order to give a committee, appointed for that purpose, time to arrange and systematize the materials which that honorable body have collected." This referred to the appointment of the Committee of Detail of which John Rutledge was chairman.

The papers also stated that, on Aug. 13, "it is said, a decision took place upon the most important question that has been agitated since the meeting of this Assembly." *Boston Gazette*, Aug. 27, 1787; this referred to the vote giving power to the House of Representatives to originate all appropriation bills.

[30] *Farrand*, III, 33, Rush to Richard Price. William Samuel Johnson wrote to his son, June 27, 1787: "It is agreed that, for the present, our deliberation shall be kept secret, so that I can only tell you that much information and eloquence has been displayed in the introductory speeches, and that we have hitherto preserved great temperance, candor, and moderation in debate, and evinced much solicitude for the public weal. Yet, as was to be expected, there is a great diversity of sentiment, which renders it impossible to determine what will be the result of our deliberation." *History of the Foundation of the Constitution* (1882), by George Bancroft, II, 430. See also *Independent Gazetteer* (Philadelphia), June 27, 1787; *Pennsylvania Packet*, June 28, July 7, 1787; *Pennsylvania Journal*, July 21, 1787; "We hear that the greatest unanimity subsists in the councils of the Federal Convention." *Independent Gazetteer*, June 16, 1787; *Connecticut Courant*, June 25, 1787; *Boston Gazette*, July 2, 1787. "We only learn, in general, that a happy and auspicious unanimity prevails in their councils." *Connecticut Courant*, July 30, 1787.

[31] "The profound secrecy hitherto observed by the Convention we cannot help considering as a happy omen, as it demonstrates that the spirit of party on any great and essential point, cannot have arisen to any height." *New York Daily Advertiser*, Aug. 14, 1787; *Pennsylvania Packet*, Aug. 22, 1787.

[32] As early as June 21, 1787, the *Independent Chronicle* in Boston said: "We understand that there exists a very great diversity of opinion among the members, and that there has been already a wonderful display of wisdom, eloquence and patriotism." See also Washington to Hamilton, July 10, 1787. Nathan Dane wrote to Rufus King, July 5, 1787: "If the Convention do not agree, at least in

NOTES

some amendments, a universal despair of our keeping together will take place. It seems to be agreed here that the Virginia plan was admitted to come upon the floor of investigation by way of experiment, and with a few yieldings on this point, and that it keeps its ground at present. The contents of this plan was known to some, I believe, before the Convention met." *Farrand*, III, 54. See Luther Martin's Letter to the Maryland Legislature (1788), (*Elliot's Debates*, I, 358): "I believe near a fortnight—perhaps more—was spent in the discussion of this business, during which we were on the verge of dissolution, scarce held together by the strength of a hair, though the public papers were announcing our extreme unanimity."

See also *Autobiography of Col. William Few* of Georgia from original MSS. in possession of William Few Chrystie, *Mag. of Amer. Hist.* (1881), VII: "The modification of the State Rights, the different interests and diversity of opinions seemed for some time to present obstacles that could not be surmounted. After about three weeks' deliberation and debating, the Convention had serious thoughts of adjourning without doing anything. All human efforts seemed to fail. Doctor Franklin proposed to appoint a chaplain and implore Divine assistance, but his motion did not prevail. It was an awful and critical moment. If the Convention had then adjourned, the dissolution of the Union of the States seemed inevitable. This consideration no doubt had its weight in reconciling clashing opinions and interests."

[33] *Farrand*, III, 64, Martin to Caswell, July 27, 1787.
[34] It is difficult to accept implicitly this statement but it is contained in a letter to Jefferson written from Philadelphia, Oct. 11, 1787, in which it is said: "The attempt is novel in history; and I can inform you of a more novel one—that I am assured by the gentlemen who served that scarcely a personality or offensive expression escaped during the whole session. The whole was concluded with a liberality and candor which does them the highest honor." *Doc. Hist.*, IV, 324.
[35] *Independent Gazetteer* (Philadelphia), Aug. 7, June 23, July 5, Aug. 9, 16, 17, 1787; *Pennsylvania Packet*

(Philadelphia), June 6, Sept. 6, July 31, 1787; *New York Daily Arvertiser*, Aug. 11, 1787; *Connecticut Courant*, Aug. 26, 1787; *Virginia Independent Chronicle*, June 20, 1787.

A letter from Virginia in *Pennsylvania Packet*, Aug. 18, 1787, said that they "impatiently wait the result of the deliberations of the collective wisdom of our vast continent now convened at Philadelphia."

See also *Independent Gazetteer*, Aug. 22, 1787; *New York Daily Advertiser*, Aug. 29, 1787; *Salem Mercury*, Sept. 4, 1787.

[36] Of the thirteen who left, there is evidence that seven approved of adoption and no evidence that any but three disapproved. The following were opposed: Luther Martin, who left Philadelphia, Sept. 4, on "indispensable business" in Maryland, but intending to return (see *Farrand*, III, 273-74). Robert Yeates and John Lansing of New York left on or soon after July 10. Of the most prominent supporters who left, George Wythe of Virginia was called home, June 4, by his wife's mortal illness; Oliver Ellsworth of Connecticut left, soon after Aug. 24; Caleb Strong of Massachusetts left, Aug. 26; Alexander Martin of North Carolina left about Sept. 1; William Pierce, William C. Houston, William Houston, Francis Dana, John F. Mercer and James McClurg were the other absentees; see *Studies of the History of the Federal Convention*, by J. F. Jameson, *Amer. Hist. Ass.* (1902), I.

[37] *Independent Gazetteer*, Sept. 21, 1787; *Salem Mercury*, Oct. 2, 1787. For Washington's speech and for Franklin's speech, on signing, as to which it was said in the newspapers: "The Address of his Excellency, Dr. Franklin to the Members of the Convention previously to this solemn transaction (a correspondent assures us) was truly pathetick and extremely sensible"—see *Connecticut Courant*, Oct. 9, 1787; *Boston Gazette*, Nov. 26, Dec. 3, 1787; and numerous other papers.

"Helvidius Priscus" (James Warren) in *Independent Chronicle*, Dec. 27, 1787, wrote: "The ancient Doctor, who has always been republican in principal and conduct, doubted, trembled, hesitated, wept and signed." Mrs. Mercy Warren in her *History of the American Revolu-*

tion, III, 363, wrote that Franklin "signed the instrument for the consolidation of the United States, with tears, and apologized for doing it at all, from the doubts and apprehensions he felt that his countrymen might not be able to do better, even if they called a new Convention."

[38] Quoted from *Pennsylvania Packet* in *Salem Mercury*, Oct. 9, 1787; *Independent Chronicle*, July 19, 1789; *Boston Gazette*, Sept. 17, 1789.

It is interesting to note that Washington gave some credit to the women of the country for the adoption of the Constitution. Writing to Mrs. A. Stockton, Aug. 31, 1788, he said: "A spirit of accommodation was happily infused into the leading characters of the continent and the minds of men were gradually prepared, by disappointment, for the reception of a good government. Nor could I rob the fairer sex of their share in the glory of a revolution so honorable to human nature, for, indeed, I think you ladies are in the number of the best Patriots America can boast." Appeals for support by the women had appeared in various papers in June 1787. "It is the duty of the American ladies in a particular manner to interest themselves in the success of the measures that are now pursuing by the Federal Convention for the happiness of America. They can retain their rank as rational beings only in a free government. In a monarchy (to which the present anarchy in America, if not restrained, must soon lead us) they will be considered as valuable members of society only as they are capable of being mothers for soldiers who are the pillars of crowned heads. It is in their power, by their influence over their husbands, brothers and sons. . ." *Independent Gazetteer*, June 5, 1787; *Salem Mercury*, June 19, 1787.

[39] George Mason wrote to his son: "The Virginia deputies (who are all here) meet and confer together, two or three hours every day, in order to form a proper correspondence of sentiments; and for form's sake, to see what new deputies are arrived, and to grow into some acquaintance with each other, we regularly meet every day at three o'clock p.m. at the State House."

[40] It may be noted that long before the proposal was made in the Convention a gentleman, writing to General

Washington, from Cambridge in Maryland, June 1, 1787, enclosing a draft drawn by another person presenting a plan for a new government said: "But disputes may arise between different States or questions of importance be created on various accounts, for the termination of which a proper power should be established. I would, therefore, vest the judicial Department in the hands of five able persons. . . . It would be their business, at stated quarterly terms, to hear and determine all disputes and controversies arising between different States, whether on account of territory, boundary, jurisdiction or other cause." *Doc. Hist.* (1905), IV, 299. The officials of the Library of Congress have been unable to identify the handwritings of either the letter or the draft. It would be interesting to ascertain what man, living near Cambridge, Md., was likely to have sent it to Washington; for the draft contains a much more detailed plan for a Supreme Court than any that had been presented in the Federal Convention up to that time.

A draft in the handwriting of James Wilson (who had argued the Pennsylvania-Connecticut Case in 1782), which was before the Committee on Detail, gave to the Senate, the jurisdiction possessed by Congress under the Articles of Confederation "in all disputes now subsisting or that may hereafter subsist between two or more States." On Aug. 6, 1787, the Committee of Detail reported by its Chairman, John Rutledge of South Carolina, a provision granting to a permanent Court compulsory jurisdiction over controversies between States but with the following exception, that boundary and territorial disputes should be settled by the Senate through a machinery of tribunals similar to those under the Confederation, appointed for each particular case. This exception was finally dropped and the Constitution was signed, containing Article III, as it now exists.

[41] *Elliot's Debates*, II, 527-58, Dec. 11, 1787. It is interesting to note that Benjamin Franklin also compared the Constitution to the project of Henry IV of France for the peace of the world. Writing to M. Grand in Europe, Oct. 22, 1787, Franklin said as to the Constitution: "If it succeeds, I do not see why you might not in Europe carry

NOTES

the project of good Henry the 4th into execution, by
forming a Federal Union and One Grand Republick of all
its different States and Kingdom, by means of a like Convention; for we had many interests to reconcile." *Doc.
Hist. of the Constitution* (1905), IV, 341; see also Wilson,
J., in *Chisholm* v. *Georgia* (1793), 2 Dallas 419, 453.
⁴²Jefferson to Smith, Nov. 13, 1787; *Popular Government* (1886), by Sir Henry Maine, p. 217; *De Tocqueville*
(1838) I, 158. While the form of federal government
evolved by the Convention, was new in the history of the
world, yet so far as the legislative and executive branches
were concerned, there were many ideas which had been
copied from the Articles of the Confederation and other
ideas which were found in various of the State Constitutions. See *The Original and Derived Features of the Constitution*, by James Harvey Robinson, *Annals of the Amer.
Acad. of Pol. and Social Science* (1890-91), I.
⁴³*Proceedings of First National Conference of Amer. Soc.
for Jud. Sett. of Int. Disputes* (1910), paper on *Development of the American Doctrine of Jurisdiction of Courts
over States*, by Alpheus H. Snow; *Proceedings of Sixth
National Conference, ibid.* (1910), paper on *The Judicial
Committee of the Privy Council*, by William Rennick
Riddell; see also *American Law Review* (1910), 161. *The
Settlement of Inter-State Disputes*, by Robert Granville
Caldwell, *Amer. Journ. of Int. Law* (1920), XIV. See also
White, C. J., in *Virginia* v. *West Virginia* (1918), 246
U.S. 565; *The Review of Colonial Legislation by the King
in Council* (1915), by Elmer Beecher Russell.
   See also *The Fedaralist No.* 80, by Alexander Hamil-
ton. As to this Imperial Chamber of the Holy Roman Em-
pire, see *Receuil des Arbitrages*, par A. de Lapradelle et
Politis. I; *Geschichte der Deutschen* (1808), by M. I.
Schmidt, IV; 364, 390; *Proceedings of Sixth National Con-
ference of Amer. Soc. for Jud. Settlement of Int. Disputes*
(1916), paper on *Execution of Judgments against States*,
by Alpheus H. Snow. *History of the Foundation of the
Constitution* (1882), by George Bancroft, II, 422.
⁴⁴Hopkinson to Jefferson, July 8, 1787, *Doc. Hist.,
IV; Jubilee of the Constitution* (1839), by John Quincy
Adams. Chief Justice White said in *Virginia* v. *West Vir-

ginia (1918), 246 U.S. 565: "The fact that in the Convention, so far as the published debates disclose, the provisions . . . were adopted without debate, it may be inferred, resulted from the necessity of their enactment, as shown by the experiences of the colonies, and by the spectre of turmoil, if not war, which . . . had so recently arisen from disputes between the States, a danger against the recurrence of which there was a common purpose efficiently to provide."

45 For an accurate expression of the action of the States, see Chief Justice Marshall in *McCulloch* v. *Maryland* (1812), 4 Wheaton 316, 410: "In America the *powers* of sovereignty are divided between the government of the Union and those of the States."

Chief Justice Chase said in *Texas* v. *White* (1868), 7 Wallace 700: "The people in whatever territory dwelling, either temporarily or permanently, and whether organized under a regular government or united by lesser and less definite relations, constitute the State."

Justice Lurton said in *Coyle* v. *Smith* (1911), 221 U.S. 559: "The people of the United States constitute one nation under one government, and this government, within the scope of the powers with which it is invested, is supreme. On the other hand, the people of each State compose a State, having its own government, and endowed with all the functions essential to separate and independent existence."

46 See Alexander Hamilton in the *Federalist*, No. 81; Bradley, J., in *Hans* v. *Louisiana* (1889), 134 U.S. 1; "The States waive their exemption from judicial power, as sovereign by origin and inherent right, by their own grant of its exercise over themselves in such cases." Baldwin, J., in *Rhode Island* v. *Massachusetts* (1838), 12 Peters 657. "If sovereignty be an exemption from suit in any other than the sovereign's own Courts, it follows that when a State by adopting the Constitution has agreed to be amenable to the power of the United States, she has in that respect given up her right of sovereignty. "Blair, J., in *Chisholm* v. *Georgia* (1793), 2 Dallas 419, 452; *World Organization and the Modern States* (1911), by David Jayne Hill. "The States as a Justiciable Person,"

NOTES

Chap. VIII, 189-90. "We may, therefore, dismiss with the most perfect assurance, the idea that submission by a sovereign State to the decision of an international Court, is in the least derogatory to its sovereignty. . . . It is an ancient maxim of the law of Nations, that a sovereign State is not amenable to a suit at law without its own consent; but it has never been held that it is in any respect derogatory to the dignity of a State to appear before a Court of Justice, to answer for its conduct and meet its responsibilities, provided in doing so, it acted freely."

[47] Chief Justice Marshall said in *Cohens* v. *Virginia* (1821), 6 Wheaton 264, 406-7, that the jurisdiction over the Court in controversies between States was retained "because it might be essential to the preservation of peace."

[48] *Moore's Digest of Int. Law*, II, 83, 298-318.

[49] For interesting discussions of sovereignty, see *Notes on Sovereignty in a State* and *Notes on World Sovereignty*, by Robert Lansing, *Amer. Journ. of Int. Law* (1907), I, (1921), XV; *The Problem of Sovereignty*, by Baron S. A. Korff, *Amer. Pol. Sci. Rev.* (1923), XVII, 404; *Sovereignty and the League of Nations*, by Geoffrey Butler, *British Year Book of Int. Law* (1920-21), p. 35; *Sovereignty*, by W. R. Bischoff, *ibid.* (1921-22), p. 122.

For opposing views of what constitutes a surrender of sovereignty and independence, see *Cong. Record, 65th Cong., 3rd Sess.*, speeches in the Senate, of Knox, March 1, 1919 (p. 4687), Reed, Feb. 26, 1919 (p. 3511), Hitchcock, Feb. 27, 1919 (p. 4417); *66th Cong., 1st Sess.*, Walsh, June 11, 1919 (p. 955); Knox, June 17, 1919 (p. 1219); Pomerene, July 21, 1919 (p. 2930); Walsh, July 28, 1919 (p. 3229); article by John P. Miller, July 28, 1919 (p. 3232); Senator McCumber said, June 18, 1919 (p. 1270): "And so we wave aloft the banners of sovereignty and independence as a scarecrow to frighten those who do not stop to consider that every compact or treaty between nations that has ever been adopted or ever will be adopted is just as much a surrender of our sovereignty or national independence as though the same treaty was made *en bloc* with all the nations in a single instrument. Whenever one nation agrees with another to do or not to do a thing which it has the right to decline to do or not to do, it does not thereby surrender its sovereignty or its independence; but it agrees in honor that it will not exercise its sovereign authority on the subject covered by the agreement during the life of the compact; . . . and the other party to the contract withholds the exercise of its sovereign power exactly in the same manner. If a nation stood upon its dignity and its right to exercise its judgment whenever it saw fit, it not only would never enter into any treaty or agreement, but at all times would, if a powerful country, be a menace to the peace of the world."

[50] See *The Boundary Disputes of Connecticut* (1882), by Clarence W. Bowen; see also *The Connecticut-New York Boundary Line*, by Simeon E. Baldwin, *New Haven Colony Hist. Soc. Proc.* (1882), II. Livingston of New York introduced a resolution in Congress, Feb. 15, 1798, that provision ought to be made for a law allowing the trial of all cases in which one or more States may be interested in such suit or suits by private parties. See *5th Cong., 1st Sess.*, 1035, 1267.

[51] See argument of Wirt in *Gibbons* v. *Ogden* (1824), 9 Wheaton 1, 184-85.

[52] See Act of June 28, 1834 (4 Stat. 708), assenting to compact between New Jersey and New York of Sept. 16, 1833; and for cases explaining this compact, see *Ex parte Devoe Mfg. Co.* (1883), 108 U.S. 401; *Central R.R.* v. *Jersey City* (1908), 209 U.S. 473; *Central R.R. of N.J.* v. *Jersey City* (1903), 70 N.J. Law 81; (1905), 72 N.J. Law 311; *N.Y. Central R.R.* v. *Hudson* (1909), 80 N.J. Law 664; (1912), 82 N.J. Law 536:

[53] Massachusetts and Rhode Island finally settled their boundaries by a compact assented to by Congress, see Act of Feb. 9, 1858 (11 Stat. 382). A compact between Massachusetts and New York ceding the district of Boston Corner to New York was assented to by Congress by the Act of Jan. 3, 1858 (10 Stat. 602). A compact between Massachusetts and Connecticut settling boundary disputes was assented to by Congress by Act of Oct. 3, 1914 (38 Stat. 727).

[54] *33d Cong., 2nd Sess.*, Jan. 17, 1855, 298, speech of Lewis Cass in the Senate; *Ohio-Michigan Boundary Line Dis-*

NOTES

pute, by Todd B. Galloway, *Ohio State Archaeological and History Soc. Rep.*, IV; *History of Ohio* (1912), by Emilius O. Randall and Daniel J. Ryan, II, 438, 446; *Scott* v. *Jones* (1847), 5 Howard 343.
[55] See especially as to this Virginia-Tennessee-Kentucky boundary line, *Russell* v. *American Association* (1917), 139 Tenn. 124.

The dispute between Washington and Oregon was settled by compact assented to by Congress by Act of June 10, 1910 (36 Stat. 881); see also *Union Fishermen's Coop. Packing Co.* v. *Shoemaker* (1920 Ore., 193 Pacific Rep. 228; *Vail* v. *Seaborg* (1922 Wash.), 207 Pacific Rep. 15; *Nielsen* v. *Oregon* (1909), 212 U.S. 315.
[56] For other cases where a State sued for protection of its citizens as *parens patriae*, see *Hudson County Water Co.* v. *McCarter* (1908), 209 U.S. 349; *Georgia* v. *Tennessee Copper Co.* (1907), 206 U.S. 230, in which Judge Holmes said that a State "has an interest independent of and behind the titles of its citizens, in all the earth and air within its domain."
[57] *International Justice*, by John W. Davis, *Amer. Bar Ass. Journ.* (1923), VIII; White, C. J., in *Virginia* v. *West Virginia* (1914), 234 U.S. 117, 121; Holmes, J., in *Virginia* v. *West Virginia* (1911), 220 U.S. 1, 36; *Missouri* v. *Illinois* (1906), 200 U.S. 496, 521; *New York* v. *New Jersey* (1921), 256 U.S. 296.
[58] Marshall, C. J., in *Cohens* v. *Virginia* (1821), 6 Wheaton 264, 378.
[59] *In Re Cooper*, 143 U.S. 503, the Court said: "In this case, His Britannic Majesty's Attorney General of Canada has presented, with the knowledge and approval of the imperial government of Great Britain, a suggestion on behalf of the claimants. He represents no property interest in the vessel . . . but only a public political interest. . . . It is very clear that, presented as a political question merely, it would not fall within our province to determine it."

See also especially *Power of a State to Divert an Interstate River, Harv. Law Rev.* (1893), VIII; *Proceedings of the Sixth National Conference of American Society for Judicial Settlement of International Disputes* (1916),

[150]

NOTES

paper by William L. Marbury; Baldwin, J., in *Rhode Island* v. *Massachusetts* (1838), 12 Peters 657; see also *United States* v. *Jones* (1890), 137 U.S. 202.

Judge Bradley said in *Hans* v. *Louisiana*, 134 U.S. 1, 15, that the Constitution made some things justiciable which were not known as such at the common law, such for example, as controversies between States as to boundary lines and other questions admitting of judicial solution. But Chief Justice Fuller in *Louisiana* v. *Texas* (1900), 176 U.S. 1, twists this statement and says that the Constitution gave to the Supreme Court only jurisdiction over controversies between States involving "matter in itself properly justiciable." There is no such limitation in the Constitution. It gives jurisdiction in all controversies between States, without any exception or limitation whatever. It is true that it is only "judicial power" which is vested by the Constitution in the Supreme Court, but "judicial power" means nothing more than power to decide a case between two parties properly before the Court. The two words "judicial power" do not contain within themselves any definition of the kind or nature of the controversy which the Court is entitled to decide.

60 *Luther* v. *Borden* (1848), 7 Howard 1; *Jones* v. *United States* (1890), 137 U.S. 202; *Pacific Telephone and Telegraph Co.* v. *Oregon* (1912), 223 U.S. 118.

61 Judge Shiras said in *Missouri* v. *Illinois* (1901), 180 U.S. 208: "It would be objectionable, and even impossible, for the Court to anticipate by definition what controversies can and what cannot be brought within the original jurisdiction of this Court."

62 See especially *What is National Honor?* (1918), by Leo Perla.

63 The Taft-Knox Treaties of 1911, contained the following phraseology: "All differences . . . relating to international matters in which the high contracting parties are concerned by virtue of a claim of right made by one against the other under treaty or otherwise, and which are justiciable in their nature by reason of being susceptible of decision by the application of the principles of law or equity." Ex-President Taft in his *The United States and Peace* (1914), Chap. III, explains this phraseology as fol-

NOTES

lows: "Those principles, of course, are principles of international law or equity . . . the words are not to be confined to the technical meaning of law and equity as those words are understood on the jurisprudence of England and the United States . . . all intended to comprehend all the rules of international law affecting the rights and duties of nations toward each other which are not mere rules of comity but are positive and may be properly enforced by judicial action."

[64] *The Classification of Justiciable Disputes*, by Philip Marshall Brown, *Amer. Journ. of Int. Law* (1922), XVI, 254: "By the way of summary, then, this problem of the classification of international disputes of a justiciable nature, while primarily a juristic problem, would appear to be involved essentially in the consideration of the actual status of international society. There would seem to exist serious grounds for doubting whether it would be possible to attempt a classification of a purely scientific character which would not have more of an academic value than a practical significance. May we not be compelled, after all, to approach this task from the political end and try by a process of elimination, that is to say, by dealing with the exceptions rather than with the rule to finally arrive at the desired goal, namely the free untrammelled administration of international justice?"

[65] See *Some Reflections on the Problem of a Society of Nations*, by Albert Kocowick, *Amer. Journ. of Int. Law* (1918), XII; *Armaments and Arbitration* (1912), by A. T. Mahan, 48.

[66] *The Outlook for International Law*, by Elihu Root, *Amer. Journal of Int. Law* (1916), X.

[67] *The American Supreme Court as an International Tribunal* (1920), by Herbert A. Smith.

[68] *Proc. Amer. Soc. for Jud. Set. of Int. Disputes* (1912), speech of George W. Wickersham.

[69] See *International Arbitrations*, by John Bassett Moore, I, 464, Salisbury to Lord Paunceforte, March, 1896, in connection with the permanent arbitration treaty between Great Britain and the United States of Jan. 11, 1897.

[70] *United States Supreme Court, the Prototype of a World Court*, by William H. Taft, *Amer. Soc. for Jud.*

Sett. of Int. Disputes (1915), Pub. No. 21. "When the suit by one State against another presents a case that is controlled by provisions of the Federal Constitution, of course, there is nothing international about it. But most controversies between States are not covered by the Federal Constitution. That instrument does not, for instance, fix the boundary line between two States. It does not fix the correlative rights of two States in the water of a nonnavigable stream that flows from one of the States into another. It does not regulate the use which the State up stream may make of the water, either by diverting it for irrigation or by using it as a carrier of noxious sewage. Nor has Congress any power under the Constitution to lay down principles, by Federal law, to govern such cases. The Legislature of neither State can pass laws to regulate the right of the other State. In other words, there is nothing but international law to govern. There is no domestic law to settle this class of cases any more than there would be if a similar controversy were to arise between Canada and the United States."

Barbour, J., said in *Lessee of Marlatt* v. *Silk* (1837), 11 Peters 1, 23, that in case of a compact between two States, "the rule of decision is not to be collected from the decisions of either State but is one, if we may so speak, of an international character."

[71] *The American Philosophy of Government* (1921), by Alpheus H. Snow. "The Proposed Codification of International Law." See also notes in *Harvard Law Rev.* (1904), **XVII**, 316, as to prescription; *ibid.* (1910), **XXIII**, note, 355; see Brown, J., in *Downes* v. *Bidwell* (1901), 182 U.S. 244, 282; *Dorr* v. *United States* (1904), 195 U.S. 138; *Rhode Island* v. *Massachusetts* (1838), 12 Peters 657, 736-8; note in *Harvard Law Review* (1907), **XXI**, 132.

As to general principles on which interstate disputes may be settled, see especially *The Administration of Justice in the Swiss Federal Court in Inter-Cantonal Disputes*, by Dr. Dietrich Schindler, *Amer. Journ. of Int. Law* (1921), **XV.**

[72] Such a condition once prevailed even as to domestic law in England; for, as Captain Mahan has pointed out: "The early Stuart Kings, notably Charles the First, with great

NOTES

care, based their oppressive actions upon law; upon law
absolute in the sense that the progress of the nation had
rendered inapplicable, methods which in previous years
had been applicable." *Armaments and Arbitration* (1912),
by A. T. Mahan, 97-9.

[73] See especially *Wedding* v. *Meyer* (1904), 192 U.S. 573,
as to concurrent jurisdiction of Kentucky and Indiana;
Harv. Law Rev. (1909), XXII, 599.

As to concurrent jurisdiction of New York and New
Jersey, see *Central R.R. of N.J.* v. *Jersey City* (1908),
209 U.S. 473.

As to concurrent jurisdiction of Washington and Ore-
gon (especially as to salmon fisheries), see *Nielsen* v.
Oregon (1909), 212 U.S. 315; *Union Fishermen's Coop.
Packing Co.* v. *Shoemaker* (1920 Ore.), 120 Pac. 476; *Vail*
v. *Seaborg* (122 Wash.), 207 Pac. 15; *Columbia River
Packers Ass.* v. *McGowan* (1909), 172 Fed. 991.

As to concurrent jurisdiction of Tennessee and Arkansas
(liquor sale on Mississippi River), see *Couch* v. *State*
(1918), 140 Tenn. 155.

As to concurrent jurisdiction of Mississippi and Arkansas (liquor sale on ferry boat on Mississippi River), see
State v. *Cunningham* (1912), 102 Miss. 237.

As to concurrent jurisdiction of Kentucky and Missouri
(liquor on Mississippi River), *Lemore* v. *Com.* (1907),
127 Ky. 480.

For concurrent jurisdiction of Iowa and Illinois (house
of ill fame on Mississippi River), *Iowa* v. *Mullen* (1872),
35 Iowa 199.

It may be noted that in several Acts of Congress admitting new States into the Union, this concurrent jurisdiction was imposed upon and accepted by the States, see
citations in *State* v. *Cunningham* (1912), 102 Miss. 237.

[74] *Barron* v. *Baltimore* (1833), 7 Peters 243; *Holmes* v.
Jennison (1840), 14 Peters 540, 614; *Virginia* v. *Tennessee* (1877), 94 U.S. 391; *Wharton* v. *Wise* (1894), 153
U.S. 155; Story, J., in *Poole* v. *Fleeger* (1837), 11 Peters
185; *Union Branch R.R.* v. *East Tenn., etc., R.R.* (1853),
14 Ga. 327; *Fisher* v. *Steele* (1887), 39 La. Ann. 447; *Mc-
Henry County* v. *Brady* (N.D. 1917), 163 N.W. 540. See
also *Story's Com. on the Constitution*, Sections 1402, 1403;

[154]

NOTES

Watson on the Constitution (1910), I, 845-9; 3 *Op. Atty. Gen.* 661, per *Légaré*.

It is well settled that concurrent legislation of two States, constituting the same entity to be a corporation in each State, does not constitute an agreement or compact that requires the assent of Congress; see *St. Louis Ry.* v. *James* (1896), 161 U.S. 545; *Mackay* v. *N.H. & H.R.R.* (1909), 82 Conn. 73; and as to an interstate bridge, see *Dover* v. *Portsmouth Bridge* (1845), 17 N.H. 200. See especially *Reciprocal Legislation*, by Samuel McCune Lindsay, *Pol. Sci. Qu.* (1911), **XXV.**

See also *The Colorado River Problem*, by N. E. Corthell, *Amer. Bar. Ass. Journ.* (1923), **IX**; and as to the *New York Port Development Compact*, see *New York* v. *Willcox* (1921), 189 N.Y. Supp. 724.

See also *Legislation through Compacts between States*, by J. P. Chamberlain, *Amer. Bar. Ass. Journ.* (1923), **IX**; *Compacts and Agreements of States*, by Andrew A. Bruce, *Minnesota Law Review* (1918), **II**; *Interstate Controversies*, *Amer. Law Rev.* (1920), **LIV.**

[75] The Supreme Court decisions disclose but one instance of a violation by a State of its compact with another State; but this one case came near presenting a serious problem for the Court. In 1823, there was decided the case of *Green* v. *Biddle* (8 Wheaton 1), involving the compact of 1789 between Virginia and Kentucky. The case was brought, not by the State of Virginia, but by private parties whose titles to land were affected by legislation of Kentucky passed to relieve that State's land-settlers of grievous hardships but claimed by Virginia as passed in direct violation of the compact. The Supreme Court decided against the validity of Kentucky's laws; and thereupon an intense and violent outburst of indignation arose in Kentucky. So extreme was the excitement that the State Legislature passed resolutions assailing the decision and hardly stopping short of advocacy of resistance to the enforcement of the Court's judgment. Luckily cooler counsels prevailed, and the decision was ultimately accepted as law.

[76] See *The Supreme Court in United States History* (1922), by Charles Warren, I, Chap. **IX**; Taney, C. J., in *Ex parte*

NOTES

Merryman (1861), 17 Federal Cases 149; and see especially
Proc. Amer. Soc. for Jud. Sett. of Int. Disputes (1916),
paper on *Execution of Judgments against States*, by
Alpheus H. Snow.

77 As early as 1793, Edmund Randolph arguing in *Chisholm* v. *Georgia*, 2 Dallas 419, said that if pressed with
the final question: "What if the State is resolved to oppose the Execution? This would be an awful question,
indeed. He to whose lot it should fall to solve it, would
be impelled to invoke the god of wisdom to illumine his
decision. . . . I will not believe that in the wide and
gloomy theatre over which his eye should roll, he might
perchance catch a glimpse of the Federal arm uplifted.
Scenes like these are too full of horror not to agitate, not
to rack the imagination. . . . It surely does not require us
to dwell on such painful possibilities. Rather let us hope
and pray that not a single star in the American constellation will ever suffer its lustre to be diminished by hostility against the sentence of a Court which itself has
adopted. But after all, although no mode of execution
should be invented, why shall not the Court proceed to
judgment . . . and there stop. . . . But that any State
should refuse to conform to a solemn determination of
the Supreme Court of the Union is impossible, until the
State abandon her love of peace, fidelity to compact and
character."

The question as to possibility of enforcement of a decree in an interstate case was also raised in *United States*
v. *Peters* (1809); *Cherokee Nation* v. *Georgia* (1831), 5
Peters 1, in which Chief Justice Marshall said, though
dismissing the suit on other grounds, the suit "requires
us to control the Legislature of Georgia, and to restrain
the exertion of its physical force. The propriety of such
an interposition by the Court may be well questioned.
It savors too much of the exercise of political power to be
within the proper province of the judicial department."
And also see *Worcester* v. *Georgia* (1832), 6 Peters 515;
Rhode Island v. *Massachusetts* (1838), 12 Peters 657;
Piqua Bank v. *Knoop* (1854), 16 Howard 369; *Ableman*
v. *Booth* (1858), 21 Howard 506; *South Dakota* v. *North*

NOTES

Carolina (1904), 192 U.S. 286; *Virginia* v. *West Virginia* (1918), 246 U.S. 565.

[78] See especially *The State as Defendant*, by William C. Coleman, *Harv. Law Rev.* (Dec. 1911), XXXI, *ibid.*, note p. 1158; *Power of the Supreme Court to Enforce a Judgment*, *Michigan Law Rev.* (1918), XVI; *Coercing a State to Pay a Judgment*, *ibid.* (1918), XVII; *Enforcement of Judgment*, *Virginia Law Rev.* (1916), IV; *Virginia-West Virginia Controversy*, *Virginia Law Reg. N.S.* (1919), IV; *West Virginia Debt Settlement*, *ibid.* (1919), V.

[79] The case of *Kentucky* v. *Dennison* (1861), 24 Howard 66, is sometimes cited as authority for the proposition that the Court will not issue mandamus to a State Governor to carry out a duty imposed upon a State by the Constitution; but it cannot be regarded really as authority for more than the precise point decided, viz., that Article IV, Section 2, of the Constitution did not grant any coercive power to the Court. Nothing in the cases citing the Dennison Case necessarily implies any greater scope for this case; see *Taylor* v. *Taunton* (1873), 16 Wallace 366; *Ex parte Virginia* (1880), 100 U.S. 339; *Ex parte Siebold* (1880), 100 U.S. 371, 391; *Drew* v. *Thaw* (1914), 235 U.S. 432.

[80] See *Punishment of Offenders against the Laws and Customs of War*, by James W. Garner, *Amer. Journ. of Int. Law* (1920), XIV. This principle had been asserted by the Institute of International Law in its Manual adopted at Oxford, in 1880. See also *Superior Orders and War Crimes*, by George A. Finch, *Amer. Journ. of Int. Law* (1921), XV.

[81] *What is National Honor?* (1918), by Leo Perla; *Political Essays*, "The Rebellion," by James Russell Lowell, p. 131; *Heart to Heart Appeals* (1917), by William J. Bryan, p. 105; *The Arbitration Treaties and the Senate Amendments*, by William Cullen Dennis, *Amer. Journ. of Int. Law* (1912), VI; *ibid.*, VI, 167-77; *The United States and Peace* (1914), by William H. Taft: "I am glad that such treaties (Bryan's) are being made. I think that the preparation of such a report will furnish useful delay while it will stimulate the negotiation of a settlement. Of course, the step is a small one, but as far as it goes it

helps. . . . The truth is that the provisions with respect to the postponement of a year in the general arbitration treaties with France and Great Britain, which I have been discussing, was suggested to me by Mr. Bryan himself, though the provision for investigation and report was taken from the Hague Convention."

See also especially "The Value of Gaining Time," in *Unjustifiable War and the Means to Avoid it*, by Heinrich Lammasch, *Amer. Journ. of Int. Law* (1916), X; *Proc. Amer. Soc. for Jud. Sett. of Int. Disputes* (1911), speeches of W. H. Taft, J. G. Schurman, W. P. Rogers and J. H. Latane. See also *Some Reflections on the Problems of a Society of Nations*, by Albert Kocowick, *Amer. Journ. of Int. Law* (1918), XII; "There is nothing rational in the concept of time, yet it is a greater force than war itself. . . . Time is the greatest of slayers and the greatest of creators."

It is but fair to say that there is a phase of the "cooling off" treaties which has been treated as a fatal defect in their theory and practical operation by Oscar T. Crosby in his *International War, its Causes and its Cure* (1919), p. 41: "In many disputes, mere delay will actually constitute a forfeiture of the claim of one of the parties; and further, mere delay is often believed to carry with it the forfeiture of the claim of both parties. Consequently to admit delay beyond that which has usually preceded the failure of diplomatic relations will be considered by one or both parties as a complete yielding of his contention. A whole category of international irritants—namely the rights and wrongs of neutrals and belligerents—fairly bristles with occasions in which delay may mean surrender."

[82] Voltaire to the Prince Royal of Prussia, Aug. 23, 1736, *Letters of Voltaire; War and a Code of Law*, by John Dewey, *The New Republic*, Oct. 24, 1923.

[83] *Proc. Amer. Soc. for Jud. Sett. of Int. Disputes* (1915), address of James Brown Scott, p. 23; see address of Samuel Chiles Mitchell, p. 63, speaking of "a practically unbroken line of precedents"—471 cases of arbitration in the nineteenth century and 125 in the twentieth century.

[84] Translation of an inscription on a stone in the Imperial

NOTES

Turkish Museum in Constantinople furnished to Rev. James L. Barton, Secretary of the Foreign Department of the American Board of Commissioners for Foreign Missions.